P-38 Light
of the ETO

SERIES EDITOR: TONY HOLMES

OSPREY AIRCRAFT OF THE ACES • 19

P-38 Lightning Aces of the ETO/MTO

John Stanaway

OSPREY
AEROSPACE

Dedication
For Jeff Ethell, who loved the P-38 so much . . .

First published in Great Britain in 1998
by Osprey, an imprint of Reed Consumer Books Limited
Michelin House, 81 Fulham Road, London SW3 6RB
and Auckland, Melbourne, Singapore and Toronto

© 1998 Osprey Publishing
© 1998 Osprey Publishing/Aerospace Publishing Colour Side-views

ISBN 1 85532698 1

Edited by Tony Holmes
Page design by TT Designs, T & S Truscott
Cover Artwork by Iain Wyllie
Aircraft Profiles by Tom Tullis
Figure Artwork by Mike Chappell
Scale Drawings by Mark Styling

Printed in China

EDITOR'S NOTE
To make this best-selling series as authoritative as possible, the editor would be extremely interested in hearing from any individual who may have relevant photographs, documentation or first-hand experiences relating to the elite pilots, and their aircraft, of the various theatres of war. Any material used will be fully credited to its original source. Please write to Tony Holmes at 10 Prospect Road, Sevenoaks, Kent, TN13 3UA, Great Britain.

CONTENTS

Sometime during the course of the war in Europe, German aircrew prisoners of war were surveyed as to the fighter types that they would most and least least prefer to meet in combat. Not surprisingly, the majority chose the Spitfire as the type they would least like to encounter, whilst the P-38 Lightning was selected as the fighter they would prefer to engage.

Unfortunately the reason for this preference was not recorded, but the fact that the P-38 was identifiable at a greater distance (meaning that it was easier to both stalk and avoid), and the natural tendency of pilots flying single-engined fighters to feel a sense of superiority over multi-engined aircraft, must have been deciding factors in the view of German pilots. Moreover, the P-38 was often encountered in inferior numbers, thus ensuring the enemy an advantage during the engagement – indeed, by the time more Lightnings became available in June 1944, the decision had already been made to transfer the type out of the Eighth Air Force.

That the P-38 often flew operations at a disadvantage is a fact not unknown to either side of the conflict. That there were fewer Lightnings than any other American fighter was a fact mitigated by the worldwide demand for the P-38. Also, the Lightning was the only USAAF fighter type committed to operations over northern Europe powered by the Allison V-1710 engine, which proved so unreliable in the cold and damp conditions that the already modest force was further reduced in number.

For all its disadvantages, both real and psychological, the P-38 *did* spread a great deal of apprehension amongst Axis airmen and soldiers, especially in North Africa and the Mediterranean. Throughout the duration of the war, all sane Axis soldiers and aircrew expressed a healthy respect for the armament of the Lightning, which lived up to the fighter's popular name at least thanks to the murderous concentration of fire emanating from the battery of four .50-calibre machine guns and single 20 mm cannon fitted in the nose of the aircraft. German pilots also expressed surprise at the way the P-38 could pull into a zoom climb without the aid of a dive or full power application. Some opponents even learned to be wary of the Lightning's ability to turn almost within its own track and reverse positions with a pursuing fighter at altitudes below 25,000 ft.

Whatever the relative merits of the P-38 in combat against the Axis air forces over Europe and the Mediterranean, the fighter's pilots and groundcrews felt fervent affection for the twin-engined Lockheed design. The dedication of those men who first took the P-38 into combat in North Africa finally blossomed into a fighting record that boasted 37 aces by the end of 1943 – a figure higher than for any other USAAF fighter type in the desert war. Indeed, so successful was the P-38 in-theatre that the 82nd Fighter Group (serving with the Fifteenth Air Force over Italy and southern Europe) held the USAAF scoring record with more than 500 aerial victories for a number of months before ultimately being overtaken by the more numerous Mustang groups in March 1945.

USAAF pilots who flew the P-38 against the European Axis exhibited a combination of eagerness, dedication, skill and impudence in the face of a remorseless enemy. From the pioneers of *Torch* to the scrapping youngsters who relentlessly hunted the Luftwaffe in the air and on the ground in the spring of 1945, the P-38 aces played their part in the Allied victory.

PIONEER P-38 ACES

T he P-38 was involved in the first successful aerial engagement between an American unit and the Luftwaffe when, on 14 August 1942, fighters of the 33rd Fighter Squadron (FS) encountered a four-engined Focke-Wulf Fw 200 Condor on patrol off the coast of Iceland and succeeded in damaging the aircraft. According to the official version (disputed by several eye-witnesses), Lt Elza E Shahan of the 27th FS observed the combat from above and swooped down in his P-38 to finish off the stricken German reconnaissance bomber. Whichever squadron delivered the mortal blow, Shahan was credited with a half-kill and the P-38 secured its place in history as having achieved the USAAC's first aerial victory against the Luftwaffe in World War 2.

During June/July 1942 the 1st FG deployed to England using the long-range capabilities of the P-38F to cross the Atlantic. In August another batch of Lightnings was flown along the same route via Labrador, Greenland and Iceland. Of the 186 aircraft that set out 179 successfully made the trip, and the first operational sorties from England were subsequently flown between 28 August and the weeks immediately prior to the November invasion of North Africa (Operation *Torch*). The P-38 would enjoy its first successes, and betray its faults, while generating its first aces over the deserts of Algeria and Tunisia.

The two squadrons of the 14th FG (the 37th and 48th FSs, which left the 50th FS in Iceland) were the first to become operational on 11

A quartet of anonymous P-38Fs fly in tight line astern formation for the camera over southern California in July 1942. Early-build Lightnings were heavily utilised in the training role by newly-equipped fighter groups prior to embarking overseas for the conflict in far-off North Africa

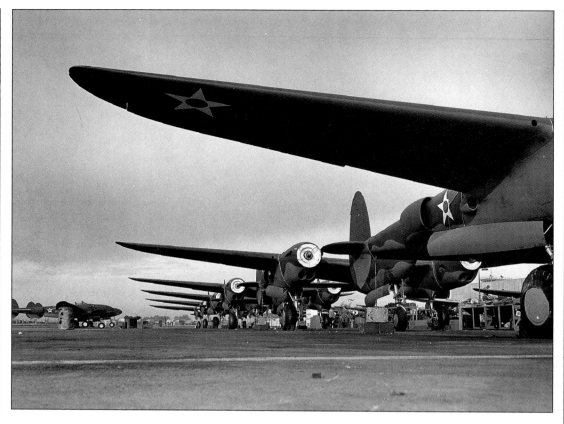

November 1942. On that day the group flew its premier mission and, according to group records, encountered enemy aircraft for the first time. The first opportunity for heavy scoring came 13 days later when the 49th FS accounted for approximately 11 aerial victories and several ground claims. Lts Virgil Lusk and James Butler were each credited with four Savoia-Marchetti SM 81 Pipistrello transports, the former pilot having almost achieved the highly coveted 'ace in a day' status when he was awarded a fifth SM 81 as probably destroyed – intriguingly, the squadron's Daily Intelligence Report actually credits Lusk (who was subsequently killed in a flying accident near NAS San Diego in P-38G-13 43-2307 on 9 March 1943) with the fifth kill!

On 28 November another 14th FG pilot almost became an 'ace in a day'. Lt Ervin Ethell of the 48th FS was on a reconnaissance mission over Tunisia when his flight bounced an escorted group of German transport aircraft. Flying on Ethell's wing that day was Lt Carl Skinner, while Lts James Butler and Redmond Evans of the 49th FS completed the flight that encountered the Ju 52/3ms, and their quartet of escorting Bf 109s, over Lake Bizerte.

Exploiting their height advantage, the American pilots dived into the enemy formation and Ethell swiftly downed four Ju 52/3ms and probably destroyed a Bf 109 that was after Skinner. The latter pilot was actually attacked by two Messerschmitts (later confirmed as Bf 109Gs from II./JG 53), one of which was shot up so badly by Ethell that it was last seen smoking and shedding pieces as it disappeared behind a hill. Despite the efforts

The associated caption for this superb Lockheed official photograph, released in July 1942, read as follows;

'DESIGN FOR VICTORY — Resembling winged monsters from Mars, these warplanes of revolutionary design are very much part of today's war in the clouds. They are Lockheed "Lightning" P-38's and rest on one of many Lockheed assembly lines awaiting final touches before joining other "Lightnings" in the fight for freedom. The P-38, super-streamlined and supercharged, is the world's fastest airplane, designed specially to intercept and destroy high-flying enemy bombers before they can unload their bombs on vital objectives. The nacelle in the middle of the center-section carries the pilot-gunner of this speedy fighter. It is a one-place machine, powered by two Allison engines. The "Lightning's" twin booms and twin rudders give it greater stability and streamlining.'

These E-models have been adorned with the old pre-12 May 1942 national marking (*via Aeroplane*)

of his squadronmate, Carl Skinner was shot down by the remaining German fighter, and James Butler also failed to return. Postwar research tends to suggest that they were the victims of Leutnant Gunther Seeger and Oberfeldwebel Stefan Litjens.

Three Lightning pilots had now scored a quartet of kills, but officially at least, none of them would go and achieve that all important fifth victory. However, another 14th FG pilot scored a signal kill (a Ju 88) on 28 November 1942, and he *would* subsequently go on to attain ace status – Lt Virgil Smith of the 48th FS was credited with a further four kills and one damaged by 12 December, thus becoming the first P-38 ace in the process.

Meanwhile, the 1st FG had flown out to Algeria from England, initially with just the 27th and 94th FSs, although the group eventually returned to full strength when the 71st FS eventually arrived in North Africa. Twenty-four hours after Lt Ethell had led his flight on its successful

Premier P-38 ace Lt Virgil Smith of the 48th FS/14th FG is seen posing in front of his P-38F-1 *"KNIPTION"* in England during the autumn of 1942. Within weeks of this photo being taken, Smith, and the rest of the 14th FG, were embroiled in the battle for North Africa (*Ilfrey*)

reconnaissance mission into Tunisia, both the 1st and 14th FGs encountered German aircraft once again, the groups' pilots being credited with two Bf 110s and two Ju 88s destroyed. Future aces Lt Jack Ilfrey and Capt Newell Roberts made their first claims on this mission, whilst Virgil Smith claimed to have damaged a *Zerstörer*.

A certain amount of confusion attends this mission in the light of Twelfth Air Force rethinking of victory claims. Jack Ilfrey remembers firing and getting hits on both Bf 110s engaged that day, and can also recall seeing Virgil Smith damage at least one of the German twin-engined fighters. However, sometime later in the war some authority within the USAAF decided to drop fraction credits for Twelfth Air Force victories and duly granted full credit for the 48th FS claim to another pilot, thus denying Smith any victory claim at all. The 94th FS claim, on the other hand, has remained divided between Roberts and Ilfrey in spite of the policy change.

The 1st and 14th FGs saw much action in the final weeks of 1942, and whilst the American pilots enjoyed numerous successes in battle, they also learned painful lessons at the hands of their battle-seasoned German and Italian opponents. Losses were suffered on the ground as well as in the air, for the 14th FG had nine of its precious P-38Gs destroyed in raids by Ju 87s and Ju 88s on its Maison Blanche base, in Algeria, on 16 and 20 November.

Both groups continued to suffer mounting casualties into 1943, for not only were inexperienced P-38 pilots having to face combat-hardened foes, they were being forced to do so from a numerically inferior position due to the paucity of Lightnings in North Africa. The Allies were committed to a broad front in-theatre, and the four (later five) P-38 squadrons were expected to not only patrol the area but also provide tactical ground attack support and, eventually, fighter escort for heavy bombers that were beginning to strike at strategic targets. North Africa was given a priority in allocation of the P-38, but even with almost total commitment of the fighter, there were simply not enough aircraft available to complete the various mission requirements.

Nevertheless, operations did continue, and the P-38 pilots slowly began to make their presence felt. For example, on 30 November 1942 single Bf 109 kills were claimed by Virgil Smith (his second confirmed victory) and Capt Joel A Owens, who also damaged another Messerschmitt fighter to register the first victories for the 27th FS – this was also the latter pilot's first encounter with the enemy.

On this historic occasion 16 P-38s of the 27th FS had escorted B-17s (of the 97th Bomb Group) sent to attack a naval base at Bizerte, in Tunisia. The bombers had already turned for home when Owens noticed a Bf 109 coming up fast through a hole in the cloud. Somehow the Lightning pilot collected himself after the excitement of seeing his first enemy fighter, and diving to close range scored telling hits around the wingroot and cockpit which sent the German aircraft rolling out of sight into the clouds below.

While he was climbing back to rejoin the bombers another Bf 109 was observed by Owens off to his left. The enemy fighter was just positioning itself for an attack on the Flying Fortresses when the 27th FS pilot slipped in directly behind it and shot the Messerschmitt down.

Cadet Virgil Smith is seen apparently ready and eager for operational life whilst undertaking his flying training in 1941. He was finally rated a pilot at Luke Field, in Arizona, just five days after the Pearl Harbor raid had plunged America into World War 2 (*Ilfrey*)

Capt Owens had followed the 1st FG out to North Africa 15 days prior to scoring his first kill, having flown at low level from RAF Chivenor, in Devon, across the Bay of Biscay and down into North-West Africa during the long flight.

On 2 December a flight of 94th FS P-38Gs flew a fighter sweep to Gabes, in Tunisia, which netted six kills, four of which were split evenly between future aces Jack Ilfrey and Newell Roberts. The latter pilot had led the sweep, with Ilfrey heading up the second element and Lts William Lovell and Richard McWherter flying as wingmen for the respective element leaders. The four P-38s thoroughly strafed the Faid Pass before continuing 'on the deck' to the port town of Sfax, where everything looked peaceful and a warship was spotted anchored in the harbour.

Pressing on on to Gabes from the north, the P-38 pilots saw a number of Bf 109s in the throes of scrambling from the airstrip as they arrived overhead. Roberts called out the enemy fighters to Ilfrey over the radio and the P-38s swiftly climbed to 1000 ft in what seemed like seconds, before plunging down into the enemy formation. Taking full advantage of their superior speed and height, each of the P-38 pilots claim a German fighter destroyed on the initial pass.

Roberts 'bagged' his first victim with a burst from dead astern at close range, describing the result of his fire in the following extract from his Form D – 'I hit the third one, giving it a long burst, and saw it blow up in the air'. Parts of the fighter scattered in all directions and some pieces hit Roberts's P-38, but he nevertheless made a hard turn to the left and shot down a second Messerschmitt ('I hit another Me 109 at about 200 ft and saw heavy black smoke pouring from it – Lt McWherter saw this plane crash to the ground') that he had managed to get into his sights.

After shooting down his first Bf 109, Jack Ilfrey made the mistake of turning through 180°, which duly brought him face to face with a second Messerschmitt fighter in the process of taking off. Rapidly taking aim, the Lightning pilot managed to shoot the German fighter down, but not before his opponent had shot up the P-38's left engine. Two more Bf 109s then latched onto Ilfrey's tail after the intrepid pilot had managed to outturn another Messerschmitt despite the damage to his left engine. The American pilot somehow avoided the enemy gunfire long enough (his comment afterward was 'Nothing in life is so exhilarating as to be shot at and missed!') for Bill Lovell to come around and shoot the two German fighters off his comrade's tail. Jack Ilfrey became understandably enthusiastic about Bill Lovell at that point, and although he tried to confirm at least one of the Messerschmitts for his rescuer, the official record of the day only granted him one destroyed and a second Bf 109 damaged.

Joel Owens scored his second victory whilst escorting 301st Bomb Group (BG) B-17s on a raid to Bizerte just two days later. Flying 20 miles southwest of the target at 19,000 ft, the 27th FS pilot spotted a battle-damaged Flying Fortress being set upon by enemy fighters.

With his wingman, Lt Lee Mendenall, following behind, Owens rapidly closed on a Bf 109 that had just completed its run on the bomber and was turning into the attacking P-38s. Firing five bursts from head-on, the Lightning pilot saw strikes from 500 yards until he broke off at about 100 yards. Owens could not, however, confirm his kill as his attention was immediately diverted by other Messerschmitt that had arrived on the

Although Virgil Smith is officially recognised as being the premier P-38 ace, this man came mighty close to achieving the coveted accolade in a single sortie on 28 November 1942. Ervin Ethell of the 48th FS/14th FG claimed four confirmed aerial victories and one probable on that date, and later wenton to unofficially destroy a further ten aircraft on the ground. He is seen here in his cadet days (*Jeff Ethell*)

scene. All was not lost though for former 27th FS CO, Maj John Welt-man, saw the stricken fighter go down in flames just as he attacked yet another Bf 109. Owens' kill was doubly confirmed some weeks later when one of the grateful B-17 gunners made a delayed report that he saw the enemy fighter hit the ground and burst into flames.

FIRST P-38 ACE

Sometime after the North African campaign had been completed the Twelfth Air Force inexplicably changed its policy concerning the award-ing of shared aerial victories. In the general shuffle of credits, the totals for 1942 were modified to affect the dates that certain P-38 pilots achieved their fifth victories. As mentioned earlier, Newell Roberts participated in the shooting down of six enemy aircraft between 29 November 1942 and 9 February 1943, and despite the policy change, he retains half-credit for the Bf 110 he shared with Jack Ilfrey on 29 November and an Italian Cant Z 1007 he helped destroy with another 94th FS pilot on 12 December. Thus, he is officially credited with five aerial victories.

Jack Ilfrey has always maintained that he scored his fifth and sixth vic-tories – a pair of Fw 190s – during a bomber escort mission on 26 Decem-ber 1942 (thus making him the premier P-38 ace), although officially these count as only his third and fourth *full* kills. Virgil Smith was origi-nally listed with two Bf 109s, a Ju 88 and a one-third credit for a Ju 52 that he attacked with two other pilots on 7 December 1942 before he claimed a Fw 190 five days later. Even with the half-credit for the Bf 110 on 29 November, he would have been credited with 4.83 victories under the old policy. He also claimed another Bf 109 on 28 December to give him ace status under any form of accounting.

However, the revised crediting gave him a full kill for the Ju 52 claimed on 7 December, thus making him an ace when he scored his Fw 190 vic-tory on the 12th. Far from being bitter about this revision of scores, Jack Ilfrey enthusiastically endorsed the status of his old aviation cadet class-mate, and fellow Texan, Virgil Smith as the first P-38 ace of the war. Since both of these pilots were pioneers in the deployment of the P-38 fighter against the European Axis powers, it is fitting that they should be the first to be recognised as successful fighter aces. What follows is a brief bio-graphical appraisal of their careers.

Virgil H Smith grew up in McAllen, Texas, and was enrolled in the first Civilian Pilot Training Program whilst still at college. He was selected for the Army Air Corps (later Army Air Forces) Cadet Program in April 1941, and graduated in the class of 41-1 at Luke Field, Arizona, on 12 December 1941. Smith joined the 14th FG's 48th FS in time to fly across the Atlantic to England with the group during the summer of 1942. After completing a handful of missions in western Europe, he moved with the 48th to North Africa in support of the *Torch* landings. After gaining his final victory on 28 December, Smith was involved in yet another combat 48 hours later near Gabes in which his P-38F was severely damaged. Whilst attempting to crash-land the stricken fighter, Smith struck a ditch and his aircraft exploded, killing him instantly. The USAAF's first P-38 ace was buried on New Year's Day 1943 in the European cemetery at Constantine, and then later reinterred in McAllen, Texas.

Virgil Smith's fellow Texan, Jack Ilfrey, was perhaps the paradigm

American fighter pilot, being both brave and unruly, and yet affable and skilled at the same time. Many of his commanders reported being happy to have a pilot of his calibre under their direction, yet at the same time felt uneasy at the daredevil risks he took in the air, or the lack of discipline he showed on the ground. After Jack had been demoted for some wild indiscretion with the 20th FG in England later in the war, his commander wrote a letter on his behalf requesting that his rank be reinstated lest an operational squadron be led into combat by a second lieutenant!

Ilfrey almost spent the war in internment when he and several other P-38 pilots were forced down in neutral Portugal whilst enroute to North Africa from south-west England. A malfunctioning fuel system had resulted in a hasty landing in Portugal during the flight to North Africa in November 1942. Following his unexpected arrival, Ilfrey was prevailed upon by his 'hosts' to demonstrate the controls of the then top secret P-38 that he flew – an armed soldier trained his weapon on the pilot in the cockpit to discourage any attempt to fly the P-38 away.

Ilfrey, however, was just reckless enough to depend on what he knew about his Lightning's sudden acceleration as soon as the throttles were advanced for taxying. He pointed out each feature of the fighter's behaviour as he started the engines and worked them up to the point of moving the aircraft. Without any warning, Ilfrey advanced the throttles and swept the observers off the wings when the aircraft lurched forward. Ignoring the standard take-off protocol, he hastily urged his P-38 into the air while the excited Portuguese made futile gestures at the impertinent American as he roared into the air, and back into the war.

Having survived 142 combat missions, Jack Ilfrey returned to civilian life after the war and worked quietly for many years as a banker in his

The irrepressible Jack Ilfrey stands by one of his P-38s in North Africa. At any moment his impish smile would cross his face, and German pilots or American commanding officers alike would be wise to take care! Despite perhaps being the unwitting victim of revisions to the Twelfth Air Force's kill credit policy post-North Africa, Ilfrey freely acknowledges that his old friend Virgil Smith was the first P-38 ace of World War 2 (*Ilfrey*)

Capt Newell Roberts of the 94th
FS/1st FG was one of the first aces
of the North African campaign,
having scored five kills by 9
February 1943. Capt Roberts
became Dr Roberts after the war,
following the completion of courses
at the University of California, the
University of Liverpool and finally
Baylor University in Texas (Roberts)

native Texas. He later moved into in real estate, and in 1979 wrote of his wartime experiences in his autobiography, titled after the P-38 that he used later with the 20th Fighter Group in England, the aptly named *Happy Jack's Go Buggy*.

Interestingly enough, all of the North African aces used the same P-38s that they brought down with them from England throughout their initial combat period. All were P-38F-1 models, and they that stood up surprisingly well to the Bf 109F/Gs and Fw 190s they encountered. P-38Gs began to appear at the beginning of 1943, and they eventually equipped all three Mediterranean Lightning groups until about the middle of the year when H-models arrived in-theatre.

It was an ironic feature of the Mediterranean air war that priorities forced P-38 units to use older variants well after other theatres had adopted advanced types – some new pilots in the 1st, 14th and 82nd FGs were more than a little surprised to find that they had been assigned older G- and H-models upon their arrival in the Mediterranean when they had left brand new P-38J/Ls behind in stateside training units!

Another pioneer P-38 pilot to attain Lightning ace status in North Africa was Capt Newell Orville Roberts, who was also a Texan, albeit transplanted from Indiana where he attended Purdue University. As mentioned earlier in this chapter, according to available records Roberts shared the Bf 110 with Jack Ilfrey on 29 November 1942, and got two Bf 109s three days later before he shared in the destruction of a Z 1007 with former 94th FS CO, Maj Glenn E Hubbard, on 12 December to give him more than three confirmed victories by the end of the year. He was credited with a further two aerial victories (both Bf 109s) on 7 and 9 February 1943 to make him a full-fledged ace, and claimed two more Messerschmitt fighters as probably destroyed and damaged. Roberts also participated in ground strafing raids against a large airfield discovered southwest of Tripoli on 8 January 1943 – he actually led two follow-up missions on this target which resulted in the destruction of a number of aircraft on the ground. Newell Roberts won the Distinguished Flying Cross with four Oak Leaf Clusters as a result of his successes.

The last of the pioneer P-38 aces to score five kills was Joel Owens, who, after securing early scores for the 27th FS in November/December 1942, failed to achieve his next victory until the last day of January 1943 – by

This unique shot, taken in May 1943 following the 14th FG's return to combat after a three-month reorganisation period, shows, from left to right, Lt Col Troy Keith (Group Commander), leading American World War 1 ace Eddie Rickenbacker, C L Tinker and early P-38 ace Maj Joel Owens (Deputy Group Commander) (*Owens*)

which time he had been made commander of the squadron. Having escorted a large formation of 17th BG B-26 Marauders on an uneventful raid on the town of Gabes, Owens was just about to break off the mission and return to base when a flight of Bf 109s bounced the Lightnings before a warning call could be given.

As the fighters split up an a wild manoeuvring battle ensued over several thousand feet, Owens saw his chance to attack two of the Messerschmitts. Instructing his element leader to take the fighter on the left while he took the one on the right, he dived down and lined up his intended victim in his gunsight. However, his fire flew wildly past the skidding target, leaving Owens to surmise that his foe had had plenty of experience duelling with Tomahawks, Kittyhawks and Hurricanes of the Desert Air Force, for his evasive manoeuvre was to pull straight up into a zoom climb. Rather than leaving the P-38 behind, this tactic only saw the Lightning close even more rapidly, which must have horrified the German pilot. Owens got off a few shots before the enemy fighter stalled out and went into a dive. Recovering several thousand feet closer to the desert floor, the Bf 109 pilot once again tried to outclimb the Owens, but this time the American centred his fire on the fuselage of the fighter and the *Jagdflieger* was obliged to jettison his canopy and take to his parachute.

Owens later transferred to the 14th FG to serve as its Deputy CO, and whilst fulfilling this role he scored his final victories – two more Bf 109s – on 10 May 1943. Following his tour of duty in North Africa, Owens went on to complete a further spell in the frontline flying P-38s in the European theatre with the Ninth Air Force's 370th FG. Even though he scored the requisite fifth victory late in the North African campaign, he is still counted as one of those pioneer P-38 aces of the initial operational period.

15

DESERT WAR

By the end of January 1943 the 14th FG had been worn down by the heavy demands of its arduous mission schedule. Used primarily in the ground attack/support role, the group had lost 32 of its original complement of 54 pilots, and had just seven operational P-38s to its name when relieved on 28 January by the Lightning-equipped 82nd FG. The 14th FG was pulled out of the frontline and eventually allocated an additional unit, the 37th FS (formerly with the 55th FG). By the time the group returned to action in May, the North African campaign was over, and it turned its attentions instead to operations over the Mediterranean.

Despite suffering appalling losses, the combat record of the 14th FG was nevertheless impressive when the heavy odds against which it flew are taken into account – 62 Axis aircraft were claimed between 21 November and 23 January. On the latter date 16 14th FG P-38s bounced a number of German aircraft taking off from an airfield near Mendenine, shooting down a solitary Bf 109 before a general mêlée ensued in which six of the Lightnings and a number of other Axis aircraft were lost. Due to the feroc-

Seen flying over the southern Pacific in early 1942, a four-ship of heavily-weathered 82nd FG P-38Es formates beneath the open bomb-bay of a Hudson bomber for Lockheed photographer Eric Miller. The group undertook a rigorous training programme prior to being sent firstly to England in the autumn, and then on to North Africa in the New Year

The mangled wreckage of Lt Irvin Ethell's P-38F-1 *TANGERINE* is examined by Luftwaffe personnel soon after it was shot down whilst being flown by another a pilot from the 48th FS. Note the right gun bay panel which carries the aircraft's nickname (*Jeff Ethell*)

ity of the engagement, the American pilots were understandably too occupied to witness their victims crashing. Despite the 14th FG enduring near-crippling losses in both men and machinery, in the final analysis the determination of the group's crews justified its presence in the desperate struggle of the early desert war.

The shortage of serviceable P-38s in-theatre had been felt as soon as late December 1942, when the call went out for all available Lightnings in England to be rushed to the area. The 82nd FG responded to the call, being posted from St Eval, in Cornwall, to Tafaroui, in Algeria, just prior to Christmas. Flying their P-38s via the Bay of Biscay, a number of pilots engaged the enemy for the first time on 23 December whilst en route to North Africa. Four Ju 88s bounced the 95th FS, and its A-20 navigation leader, from the rear, quickly shooting down the Havoc and the trailing P-38 of Lt Earl Green – the latter pilot survived the incident and subsequently evaded both capture and internment.

Reacting quickly to the carnage occurring behind him, formation leader Maj Bob Kirtley wheeled around and turned head on into the German attackers. His wingman stayed with him as he followed the Ju 88s after they had broken off the engagement and dived into the clouds below. When the major came out of the undercast he found himself directly behind one of the fleeing fighter-bombers, so he closed to within

Premier P-38 ace Lt Virgil Smith is seen posing beside his P-38 on 14 December 1942 – just two days after scoring his all important fifth victory. As detailed in chapter one, Smith's final tally of six was not confirmed until years after the war when he was controversially given full credit for shared victories scored early on in his brief frontline career (*USAF*)

Factory-fresh P-38Gs have their engines run after being re-assembled following a precarious Atlantic crossing by freighter. This photograph was taken at Lockheed's British Reassembly Division, sited at Liverpool's Speke Airport, on 16 January 1943, each fighter spending between six and eight hours on the line having their engines checked at various rpm to ensure that they had withstood the sea voyage. Once passed fit for service, these Lightnings were rushed south to North Africa in order to relieve the chronic P-38 shortage at the front

100 yards of his target in order to make the most of the meagre 50 rounds per .50-calibre gun that he had been allotted for the flight – ammunition had been kept to a minimum in order to allow the Lightnings to carry more fuel for the long transit. As it turned out, the solitary burst that Kirtley managed to get off before his guns hissed empty was enough to start a fire in the left engine of the Ju 88, and the major duly watched his target glide into the sea. Lt Arthur Brodhead, who had followed Kirtley down, accounted for a second Junkers fighter-bomber.

Once safely ensconced in Algeria, elements of the 82nd FG commenced patrols over the eastern part of the North African battleground during the last days of 1942 – the group finally reassembled at Tafaroui in the first week of 1943. Fittingly enough, the first aerial victory to fall to an 82nd FG pilot in North African skies was scored by the man who would later become the group's top ace flying its most celebrated P-38. Lt William 'Dixie' Sloan of the 96th FS was part of an escort of 319th BG B-26s on what would become known as 'The Gabes Meat-run' on 7 January when he claimed one of six Bf 109s attempting an interception.

Sloan was self-effacing about his first victory, recounting in an inter-

This view, taken by a *Flight* staff photographer in December 1942, shows to good advantage the potent armament fit of the Lightning – four .50-calibre machine guns and a solitary 20 mm cannon. The armourer is seen here adjusting the belt feed of one of the machine guns (*Aeroplane*)

Another photo in the *Flight* sequence reveals the weather to be less than ideal for flying – winter mist would hardly be a problem once this Lightning arrived at its final destination – Algeria (*Aeroplane*)

view conducted many years after the war that the only reason he downed the enemy fighter was that it got in the way between him and his base at Tafaroui! On this mission Sloan used P-38F-15 43-2112 (nicknamed *"SAD SACK"*), which was the regular mount of future Lightning ace Capt Ernest Osher of the 95th FS. The latter pilot, who would go on to command this unit between 1 May and 26 July 1943, scored virtually all of his five victories in 43-2112. *"SAD SACK"* remained in the frontline until early 1944, during which time it was used by various pilots to destroy as many as 16 aircraft – a phenomenal success rate which earned it a reputation for being one of the best examples of the P-38 ever manufactured.

It seems highly likely that Capt Osher was using *"SAD SACK"* when he claimed his first victory (a Bf 109) during a bomber escort to Tunis on 29 January. Fellow 82nd FG pilot, and future ace, Lt Claude Kinsey also got a Bf 109 that had attempted to intercept the American formation – by the time the 96th FS pilot had been shot down over Cap Bon on 5 April, he had become the top P-38 ace in North Africa with seven confirmed aerial victories, two probables and one damaged.

On 30 January the Gabes area was visited once again by the 82nd FG's 96th FS, with a further eight victories being tallied. One confirmed and one probable (both Bf 109s) fell to Kinsey, an Fw 190 was claimed by 96th CO, and future seven-kill ace, Maj Harley Vaughn (his second victory) and yet another Bf 109 was credited to 'Dixie' Sloan.

In spite of these successes, the 82nd FG still had to contend with the same hardships which had all but destroyed the 14th FG. The Axis air forces continued to enjoy both numerical superiority and an edge in experience that resulted in the P-38 units suffering grievous losses and crippling battle damage. To make matters worse, the 82nd was also forced to sustain aircraft losses incurred by other Lightning operators within the Twelfth Air Force from its own limited stocks, resulting in the demand for P-38s reaching acute levels once again during the 'dark period' of January-February 1943. Spares were also in short supply, making necessary the unseemly sight of groundcrews swarming over damaged P-38s to cannibalise parts for their own worn, and near to unserviceable, aircraft.

Flying in the face of such adversities, the 96th FS opened its February scoring with an impressive seven victories for just one loss on the second day of the month. Sixteen P-38s were once again escorting B-26s of the 319th BG on an anti-shipping strike off Cape Bon when a swarm of German and Italian aircraft were encountered. The Lightnings were forced to take a defensive stand in a great Lufbery circle, with each P-38 following another for mutual protection.

Like Jack Ilfrey, 'Dixie' Sloan has been accused over the years of occasionally disrupting the strict 96th FS tactical discipline, but during this sortie all he did was simply shift his sights ever so slightly when a Bf 109 foolishly decided to enter the circle. The German fighter exploded under the concentrated weight of Sloan's fire, and every member of the circle witnessed the wreckage crash into the Mediterranean. When the Lufbery later broke up and the P-38s dashed for home, Sloan was bounced by another fighter which severely damaged his Lightning prior to being shaken off. Feeling rather vulnerable in his shot up fighter, the redoubtable young P-38 pilot was able to find cover with the very B-26 formation that he had earlier been protecting. So secure was Sloan with

A beaming Lt William 'Dixie' Sloan of the 96th FS/82nd FG poses by P-38F-15 43-2064 sometime between 2 and 15 February 1943. Sloan was surprised a few years ago by a telephone call from the leader a B-26 formation who renewed their wartime friendship by thanking him for his escort on 2 February 1943, and then jokingly chided him for stealing the Marauder pilot's victory while accepting the protection of the B-26's guns! (*USAF*)

his Marauder 'fighter cover' that he managed to shoot down an attacking Do 217 as the bombers left the target area – an event again witnessed by virtually the entire American formation.

Thirteen days later, during yet another B-26 escort, Sloan claimed his fourth Bf 109 to become the 82nd's first ace. He had been a relative 'wildcat' within the highly disciplined 96th FS, whose strict adherence to radio procedures had led to many surprise bounces of the enemy by the group's P-38s – even German veterans of the campaign remarked favourably on this aspect of the squadron's fighting prowess postwar. However, like most other high scoring fighter pilots, Sloan often went beyond the bounds of discipline in the air, resulting in him scoring victories nearly every time he met the enemy. Indeed, not only did 'Dixie' Sloan enjoy more success than his comrades in the group, he also became the top-scoring ace of the Twelfth Air Force with 12 victories and 5 damaged.

The effect of air discipline on the 82nd FG is evinced by the fact that its credited victories were divided between more than 200 pilots. Aside from Sloan's haul, only the 96th FS's Flt Off Frank Hurlbut (nine destroyed, one probable and four damaged by 2 September 1943) and Lt Charles Zubarik (eight destroyed, and one damaged by the time he was shot down and captured on 24 May 1943) scored anywhere near double figures in the Mediterranean. The 82nd FG remained the top-scoring American fighter unit in the Mediterranean (with 553 victories) for almost two years before finally being surpassed by Mustang groups in 1945.

1ST FG

January 1943 brought more strategic missions on top of the tactical runs to Gabes, Sfax and Bizerte. Whilst participating in the former, the 71st FS of the 1st FG downed two fighters over Tripoli on the 12th of the month, one of these being credited to Lt Meldrum Sears (his second kill). Squadronmate Lt Lee Wiseman claimed his first victory on 4 February, and both pilots would enjoy more success during April.

Capt Ernest K Osher and his groundcrew stand by the famed P-38F-15 43-2112/ *"SAD SACK"*, which the former used to claim most of his five victories. The veteran fighter had been credited with as many as 16 kills by the spring of 1944 (*USAF*)

Another man who would score heavily during early 1943 was Lt John Wolford of the 27th FS/1st FG, who had actually claimed his first victory (an 'Me 109E') on 3 December 1942 near Bizerte airfield whilst flying a P-38F. He lodged the following combat report for this action;

'Lt SULLIVAN and I turned left into two ME-109, which were diving from about 4 to 5000 ft above us. Lt SULLIVAN had completed his turn and I was about 100 yards behind him still turning. One ME-109 made a quick turn from his altitude, at this time about 1 to 2000 ft above us, to Lt SULLIVAN'S right and behind, and cut between Lt SULLIVAN and myself. I saw the E/A give Lt SULLIVAN one burst before I could bring my sights into line When I had turned sharply enough to bring my sights to bear, I gave the E/A a wild burst to try to turn him from Lt SULLI-VAN. Time did not permit me to line my sight carefully, because of the short distance between the E/A and Lt SULLIVAN, now about 50 yards. As I fired my cannon ran out of ammunition and two mg's jammed. Tightening my turn as much as possible, I slipped over the E/A to the right side, from which I took another shot with the two good guns. As I shot, Lt SULLIVAN started a turn to the right and the E/A followed. I observed the tracers entering the cockpit of the E/A. After the tracers entered the cockpit the E/A shook slightly and continued a gentle turn to the right, nosing down gradually. No evasive action was taken by the E/A, and the last time I saw him, he was headed straight down through the clouds, the clouds being about 3000 ft level. I could not follow him down because of the crippled condition of Lt SULLIVAN'S ship, behind which I weaved to keep off any further attack. No further attack was experienced. During my attack on the first E/A the second E/A evidently got a shot at me as I had a hole in my right wing tip, severing the navigation light wire, a glancing shot off the left wheel door, and a clean hole through one blade of the left propeller. I claim this E/A as destroyed.'

Wolford went on to add two more Bf 109s, a Fw 190 (plus a second Focke-Wulf damaged) and a Macchi MC 200 to his tally during March 1943, achieving ace status on the 23rd of the month. He was finally posted Missing In Action near Trapani on 19 May, having taken his score to five destroyed and two damaged.

Capt Darrell Welch (five kills and three damaged) was another veteran pilot of the 27th FS who claimed a Bf 109 (his second) on 23 March, and who go on to attain more victories during April. Similarly, Lt John Mackay (six kills and one probable) also downed a Bf 109 for his first score on 23 March as a precursor to more successes in April/May.

From the final days of March until the Axis surrender in North Africa on 13 May, the shrinking perimeter around Cap Bon, forced Luftwaffe transports to fly a hazardous route between Sicily and Tunisia. During April this narrow corridor offered long-ranging P-38s the opportunity to destroy 100+ aircraft – mostly Ju 52/3ms.

In the weeks prior to the 'slaughter', future Lightning aces began to score more freely. One such pilot was the 27th FS's Lt Daniel Kennedy in his colourful P-38G *THE BEANTOWN BOYS*, which he used to shoot down his first confirmed kill (an Fw 190) on 8 March. The 96th FS enjoyed great success 12 days later when it claimed 11 aircraft during an anti-shipping strike. Future seven-kill ace Lt Ward Kuentzel claimed his first two victories (Bf 109s) in P-38F-15 43-2153, whilst Claude Kinsey

Lt Gerald Rounds of the 97th FS/82nd FG flew a number of exciting missions from North Africa during the opening days of the Italian invasion. All five destroyed, one probable and two damaged claims credited to Rounds comprised Bf 109s. He particularly remembers his third victory on 24 May 1943 over Alghero airfield, on Sardinia, when he enticed a pursuing Messerschmitt to under-shoot his P-38, thus instantly switching from being victor to victim (*Gerald Rounds*)

97th FS/62nd FG pilot Lt Thomas Ace White scored a Bf 109 on 28 February 1943 for his fifth victory and an Me 210 on 11 March for his final claim. Both were scored in P-38G-10 42-12943 (*Blake*)

'made ace' in P-38G-10 42-12871 when he downed a 'single-engined two-seat Italian fighter'. Harley Vaughn also tasted success flying P-38G-5 42-12827 by downing a Ju 88, and Charles Zubarik claimed a pair of Bf 109s in his usual G-10, 42-13054.

The nature of air combat drastically changed during the first week of April as the Twelfth Air Force set about the wholesale destruction of the Luftwaffe's air transport fleet in the Mediterranean. Codenamed Operation *Flax* by the Allies, fighter patrols were set up to sever the Axis air bridge from Sicily to Tunisia. This was effectively achieved in just three days of fighting, the first combat taking place on the 5th when 50-70 transports, escorted by 30 fighters, were sighted heading for Cap Bon. The 1st FG's 27th FS waded into the formation and exacted a toll of roughly 16 aircraft for the loss of two P-38s.

Between them, John MacKay and Darrell Welch scored a good portion of the 27th's claims when they each accounted for three aircraft apiece. The latter pilot's trio of victories, comprising three Ju 52/3ms, earned him ace status, whilst MacKay claimed two Junkers transports followed by an Fw 189 twin-boom reconnaissance aircraft, which he chased inland before shooting it down – these successes took for his tally to four.

Elsewhere, the 82nd FG engaged a mixed formation of roughly 20 Bf 109s and Ju 52/3ms whilst escorting B-25 Mitchells of the 321st BG on an anti-shipping sweep. Once again the P-38 pilots seized the initiative and claimed nine transports and eight escort aircraft destroyed, but at a price – four Lightnings failed to return to base.

One of the P-38 pilots lost was Claude Kinsey, who had swiftly downed two Junkers transports in flames to raise his tally to seven victories when he felt a heavy blow to his body which he attributed to fire from the enemy escort. Even though he was badly injured and forced to fly at 350 mph low over the water to effect his escape, Kinsey managed to bale out of his stricken fighter near the Tunisian shoreline and struggle ashore. His legs were injured, he had burns on his face and he found out later that his ribs were crushed, all of which ruled out the chance of evading capture. Five Arabs quickly appeared on the beach where Kinsey was huddled and carried the wounded American to an Italian camp.

Five days later the 71st FS made its contribution to *Flax* when its pilots claimed roughly half of the 40+ Axis aircraft destroyed. During the morning patrol the squadron ran into a formation of Italian Savoia-Marchetti transports, escorted by Macchi MC 200 fighters, and by the time the P-38s were done, at least 20 transports and two fighters had been downed.

Meldrum Sears added four transports to the Ju 52/3m and Fi 156 that he had claimed in January to become the latest ace of the 1st FG, whilst Lee Wiseman 'bagged' two more Junkers tri-motors and a MC 200 to add to the Fw 190 he had claimed two months earlier. Forty-eight hours after his triple success he claimed his fifth, and last, victory (another Fw 190).

Soon after midday on the 10th the 82nd FG ran into yet another formation of 25 Ju 52/3ms, escorted by Bf 110s and Ju 88s, whilst escorting B-25s sent to bomb Cap Bon. The Lightnings claimed ten transports and three of the escorts while the B-25s also accounted for ten Ju 52/3ms.

One 97th FS pilot who achieved 'acedom' during this engagement was Lt Ray Crawford, who tore into the Junkers transports and swiftly claimed two of them to register his fourth and fifth victories. Lt Bill

Lt Jack Ilfrey and one of his groundcrew pose by various parts of *TEXAS TERROR*, alias P-38F-1 41-7587. Note that the sixth victory swastika in the top photograph has been hastily taped out, indicating that the Twelfth Air Force's policy change in crediting shared victories had already been acted upon by the 1st FG – this marking referred to a Bf 110 kill Ilfrey had split with the late Virgil Smith on 29 November 1942, the latter individual being posthumously credited with the whole victory (*both Ilfrey*)

Capt Darrell Welch's P-38F *SKY Ranger* was used by him sometime after he had scored heavily during Operation *Flax* in April 1943. Having joined the 27th FS/1st FG whilst both units were still pursuit designated in June 1941, Welch's combat tour came to an end soon after he had secured his ace status with a trio of Ju 52/3ms on 5 April (*Welch*)

Schildt of the 95th FS also got a Bf 109 to augment a Bf 110 kill scored on 31 January. Less than 24 hours later he too would be an ace.

Schildt's 95th FS took the scoring honours on the 11th. No fewer than 19 P-38s were on a *Flax* sweep when 20 transports, escorted by fighters, were sighted halfway between Sicily and Cap Bon. Two flights of P-38s tackled the escorts while the others tore into the Ju 52/3ms.

Schildt led his flight into the heart of the transports' formation and sent three of them flaming down into the sea. The scene quickly turned into one of carnage as the water seemed to be on fire with burning debris, pieces of Ju 52/3m jutting out of the water at varying angles. One transport landed intact on the surface and several crewmen were spotted clinging to the wings hoping to be rescued. Officially, the 95th downed all 20 Ju 52/3ms and seven of the escorts, including three Bf 109s, two Bf 110s (from III./ZG 26) and a solitary Ju 88, for the loss of three pilots. Schildt's trio of kills victories made him the 82nd's fifth ace.

Later that same morning the 96th FS flew a similar mission and ran into another formation of transports low over the water, duly dispatching five of them for the loss of a single P-38. One of the Ju 52/3ms was claimed by former Flt Off Frank Hurlbut, participating in his first mission since arriving from England – the young 20-year-old from Salt Lake City would eventually become the second-ranking ace of the 82nd FG. The 82nd was now the dominant USAAF fighter unit in the Mediterranean with 170+ aerial victories, and since the beginning of April P-38 pilots had claimed in excess of 100 transports, plus escorting fighters.

However, the crowning *Flax* mission was flown on 18 April when American P-40s and RAF Spitfires claimed 59 transports destroyed in a record operation. The Curtiss fighter stole further glory from the P-38 in North Africa by producing the top USAAF ace of the period in Capt Levi

Lt Bill Schildt of the 95th FS/ 82nd FG also accounted for three Ju 52/3ms, although his trio was claimed on 11 April – he was acting CO of his squadron on this particular day. Schildt completed 50 combat missions with the 95th FS before being transferred back to the USA. He subsequently spent the rest of the war flying C-54s in the Pacific (*via Blake*)

Chase of the 33rd FG, who ended the campaign with ten victories. His P-38 equivalents were Claude Kinsey of the 96th FS and Meldrum Sears of the 71st FS, both of whom scored seven kills.

THE END IN MAY

By the end of the fighting in North Africa the enlarged 14th FG had returned to the action once again, this time with a full group complement comprising three units – the 37th, 48th and 49th FSs. And although the surrender of the 250,000 Axis troops trapped on Cap Bon on 13 May had signalled the end of the Desert War, P-38 units were already ranging across the Mediterranean into southern Europe in search of the enemy.

Indeed, the 82nd FG's 95th FS claimed six Italian transports and three escort fighters south-west of Marettimo Island a full eight days prior to the Axis capitulation in Tunisia, Ernest Osher (flying *SAD SACK*) downing an SM 82 transport and a Macchi MC 200 fighter. He followed up this double success on 11 May with the destruction of a Bf 109 over Marsala, on the island of Sicily, achieving ace status in the process.

Two days prior to Osher's Bf 109 kill, the 14th FG had scored its first victories of the renewed tour when four aircraft were claimed. Amongst the successful pilots on this day was future seven-kill ace Capt Herbert Ross of the 48th FS, who was credited with the destruction of an MC 202. Twenty-four hours later it was the turn of Deputy Group CO, Maj Joel Owens, to at last 'make ace' when he added to the 14th FG's tally with a pair of Bf 109s – his first kill had been scored as long ago as 30 November 1942. He submitted the following combat report upon returning to base;

'1. While acting as leader of Big Ben (37th) Squadron escorting B-17s to Bo Rizzo A/D on 10 May 1943, the following engagements took place:

'2. I was leading a flight of six P-38s attempting to cover the withdrawal of the last group of bombers at 26,000 ft, then a red smoke shell burst and about 20 E/As appeared. One made an attack on White section and I turned into the attack. I stalled my ship and dropped about 2000 ft. I was immediately surrounded by four E/A, one of which made an attack from six o'clock. I waited until he started firing, then I broke sharply to the right then made a diving turn left and the E/A was about 150 yards in front of me. I fired two bursts and the E/A went down with a large volume of black smoke coming out underneath his engine. I did not watch the E/A, but instead turned into a new attack. I made a steep spiral dive to about 15,000 ft and levelled out, then two more E/A attacked, one from six o'clock and the other from four o'clock. I again broke to the right and followed with a vertical reversement. One of the E/A overshot me and was about a hundred yards in front of me, climbing to the left. I got on his tail and fired a long burst from 100 yards; he fell off into a spin and after about four turns of the spin he broke into flames and went into the sea. While I was watching him the other E/A made an attack and scored hits on my left rudder and radiator. I immediately went into a spin to about 4000 ft, went into some clouds and came home. The E/A did not follow.

'3. I learned when I returned to base that Lt Hendrix had seen both E/A burst into flames and fall into the sea. Claim: 2 ME 109s destroyed.'

Another pilot to secure 'acedom' in early May was Charles Zubarik of the 96th FS, whose controversial kills scored on the morning of the 5th

Lt Claude Kinsey had become the top P-38 ace in North Africa by the time he was shot down on 5 April after scoring his sixth and seventh victories – two Ju 52/3ms – off Cap Bon. Kinsey remained a PoW until escaping on 29 October 1943 and walking over a hundred miles back to Allied lines. He was subsequently posted back to the USA and saw out the remainder of the war as an instructor (*Blake*)

were achieved in rather unusual fashion . Whilst escorting B-25s north of Cap Serrat, Zubarik noticed that one of his engines was showing the early signs of trouble, so he reluctantly broke of the mission and turned back for home. He had no sooner reversed his course and set off for the 82nd FG's base at Berteaux when his engine started running normally again, so he decided to try and find his flight once more. However, rather than encountering P-38s, Zubarik ran straight into a formation of five Me 210Cs, and while he tried to get above the enemy to commence a diving attack, the Lightning pilot noticed two of the wildly manoeuvring Messerschmitts collide and fall into the sea!

He managed to stay above the remaining fighters, but wisely decided to make for home in view of their superior number, and the suspect nature of one of his engines. The troublesome Allison did eventually run away later in the flight, and Zubarik was forced to make an emergency landing in a wheat field. When he did finally coax his P-38 back into the air and affect a recover at Berteaux early in the evening, he was frustrated in his

71st FS/1st FG pilots who did well during the 10 April 1943 sweep of the transports re-live the action off Cap Bon for the camera – left to right, Lts Walter J Rivers (final total of 4 destroyed, 2 probables and 2 damaged), John L Moutier (final total of 4.5 destroyed and 2 damaged), Meldrum Sears (final total of 7 destroyed, including four Ju 52/3ms on this date) and Lee V Wiseman (final total of 5 destroyed, including two Ju 52/3ms and an MC 200 this date) (*USAF*)

Lt Charles J Zubarik officially gained his fifth victory on 13 May 1943 when he claimed an MC200 south-west of Cagliari, Sardinia. The two question marks at the right of his scoreboard signify a pair of Me 210s that he had forced to collide exactly a week prior to his Macchi kill. As these could not be confirmed by independent witnesses, the Twelfth Air Force refused to credit Zubarik with them, hence the question marks. The 96th FS/82nd FG's third-ranking ace was shot down and taken prisoner on 24 May 1943 (*James Crow via Steve Blake*)

attempts to get credit for the two colliding German aircraft. In the end he was denied these 'kills' by the USAAF, and had to settle for a pair of question marks as victory symbols on the side of his P-38 instead.

Zubarik officially confirmed his 'ace status' on 13 May when he destroyed an MC 200 south-west of Sardinia, and went on to score his sixth, and final, recognised victory on eight days later – his Bf 109 was just one of seven kills credited to the 82nd on this day. On 24 May he was shot down south of Vanafiorita airfield, fellow ace, and squadronmate, 'Dixie' Sloan violating official policy by refuelling and going back to look for Zubarik. Sadly, all he discovered was the burning wreck of a P-38G in the Sardinian scrub. When he returned home, a dejected Sloan found 'hot words and cold shoulders' for a welcome, but he was later overjoyed to hear that Zubarik was alive and a prisoner of war.

Other future aces enjoyed more luck during May, however, the 95th FS's Lt Louis Curdes adding two Bf 109s on the 19th to the trio of Messerschmitts he had claimed on only his second mission on 29 April. Frank Hurlbut got his second kill (an Fw 190) on the 20th, John MacKay of the 27th FS his fifth and sixth (and last) victories – two Bf 109s – on the 25th, future five-kill man Lt Sidney Weatherford of the 14th FG's 48th FS opened his account on the 28th (with a Bf 109), and finally Daniel Kennedy of the 27th FS finished the month with a Bf 109 on the 31st.

By the end of May 1943 P-38s were roaming all over in the western Mediterranean in search of the enemy, and within a few days they would be constantly engaging Axis aircraft over southern Europe proper.

MEDITERRANEAN WAR

The first real victories beyond the North African campaign were the seizures of the islands of Pantelleria and Lampedusa, which were surrendered by the Axis without invasion on 11 and 12 June 1943 respectively. This followed in the wake of a severe pounding by aerial forces beginning 31 May, the wavering Italian garrisons deciding to capitulate to the inevitable.

P-38s were in the forefront of the action because of their longer range, and some fruitful engagements were fought. On 18 June the 96th FS engaged the enemy whilst escorting B-25s to Sardinia, the Lightning pilots being positioned low over the water when the first six enemy fighters appeared, followed by many until the battle turned into a general mêlée. The P-38s individually climbed into the action at about 10,000 ft, claiming 16 interceptors for the loss of a single fighter and no bombers.

Amongst the successful pilots was Lt Larry Liebers, who shot down two MC 202s and a single MC 205 to become the latest ace of the 82nd FG. Frank Hurlbut claimed a Bf 109 and an Re 2001 to take his tally to four, as did Lt Edward Waters courtesy of a Bf 109, whilst Ward Kuentzel claimed a MC 202 for his third victory. Finally, 'Dixie' Sloan also got an MC 200 to raise his tally to eight.

The 82nd FG enjoyed further success during the opening phase of the invasion of Sicily, five enemy fighters falling to unit during a ground attack mission on the Gerbini airfields on 5 July. A number of German and Italian interceptors had scrambled to engage the P-38s as they left the target and reached the Sicilian coast. 'Dixie' Sloan claimed a Bf 109 and a Re 2001 to break into double figures, whilst Lt Gerald Rounds of the 97th FS claimed another Bf 109 for his fourth kill.

Once the invasion had commenced, the 82nd temporarily flew sorties from Libya under the direc-

This photo was taken around 19 May 1943, soon after Lt Louis Curdes (centre) had claimed two Bf 109s for his fourth and fifth victories. Curdes and Lts J G Oliver (left) and R Embrey (right), accounted for four Bf 109s on the 19th. The former pilot later spent time as a PoW after being downed in August 1943, but went on to fly P-51s in the Pacific following his release, and score a solitary Japanese kill – plus a USAAF C-47 that was attempting to land at an enemy airfield in error. Curdes disabled the transport, forcing it to ditch offshore and allowing its crew to be rescued by friendly forces (*USAF*)

tion of the RAF's No 320 Wing. On the day of the actual landings (10 July) the 96th FS put up another sterling display by claiming seven *Schlacht* (ground attack) Fw 190s and solitary examples of the Ju 88, Bf 109 and MC 200. 'Dixie' Sloan 'bagged' the Italian fighter to become the leading ace of the Twelfth Air Force with 11 confirmed victories, whilst Frank Hurlbut got three of the Focke-Wulfs to become an ace with seven kills. Larry Liebers also confirmed one Fw 190 and damaged two others for his sixth victory. Ward Kuentzel claimed the Ju 88 and yet another Fw 190 for victories number five and six, and Edward Waters claimed the Bf 109 for his seventh, and final, score.

It was the turn of the 14th FG to get amongst the transports once again on 18 July, P-38s of the 37th and 48th FSs chancing upon 15 Ju 52/3ms heading for Sardinia whilst they were escorting a Sunderland flying boat on a rescue mission. The Lightning pilots jumped the hapless Junkers transports and shot them all down, four falling to Lt Lloyd Hendrix (his only victories) and two to future five-kill ace Lt Paul Wilkins. Pilots of the 48th FS shared the remaining nine transports, two apiece going to future aces Sidney Weatherford (taking his overall score to four) and Capt Herbert Ross (his second and third victories).

'Dixie' Sloan got his final kill on 22 July – the day Allied troops entered Palermo – during whilst escorting B-25s sent to bomb a railroad junction at Battopaglia, on the Italian mainland. Just after the Mitchells had left the target and set their noses down for more speed, a trio of enemy fighters attempted to intercept the fleeing bombers but were quickly driven off by the 26 escorting P-38s. Two more Bf 109s quickly joined in the fray towards the rear of the bomber formation, but they too were intercepted in time by Sloan's and Kuentzel's flights – both aces closed so tightly on their targets that they could see the pilots' yellow cloth helmets. The Lightning pilots fired their guns almost simultaneously, sending both enemy fighters down in flames.

Sixteen days later ten Bf 109Gs of II./JG 77 were on a *freie jagd* (fighter sweep) just off the south-west coast of Italy when they bounced 30 Lightnings from above. Sixteen of the P-38s were from the 96th FS, and they responded so quickly that they shot down the fighter flown by Leutnant Egon Graf and damaged Unteroffizier Philipp's Messerschmitt so badly it he had to force-land at Vibo Valentia. Frank Hurlbut claimed an 'Fw 190' during this operation as his eighth victory, and is likely that his victim was Leutnant Graf.

INVASION OF ITALY

The end of August and beginning of September 1943 saw the Mediterranean-based P-38 units play an instrumental part in the return of the Allies to the European mainland via the Italian peninsula. For example, on 25 August the 1st and 82nd FGs were part of the surprise strafing mission on the airfields of the Foggia plain which resulted in over 100 claims for aircraft destroyed on the ground – Lt Joe Miller and now Maj Herbert Ross of the 48th FS also claimed an MC 202 apiece in the air. For Ross it would be his fifth (of seven) victory, while Miller would claim four with the 48th and a fifth with the British-based 474th FG in March 1945.

During the same period Lt Clarence Johnson of the 96th FS downed two Fw 190s on 20 August and two more Bf 109s on 2 September. He

Lt Clarence Johnson of the 96th FS claimed four enemy aircraft (MC 202 on 21 May 1943, two Fw 190s on 20 August 1943 and a Bf 109 on 2 September) before being posted to the 436th FS in England. He achieved 'ace status' with his new unit when he downed an Fi 156 on 22 June 1944, this victory also being the 436th's premier score. Johnson was later shot down and killed on 25 September whilst flying a P-51D-10 (*Blake*)

Lt Richard J Lee is seen wearing the DFC (the medal to the left) that he won for attacking several Italian fighters while one of his engines was disabled. He was credited with one MC 202 during the 21 August 1943 mission, later adding four more during his time with the 94th FS/1st FG (*R J Lee*)

Lt James Hollingsworth of the 37th FS (in British Guinea Base t-shirt) poses informally with his groundcrew sometime in mid-1943. Although only officially credited with three confirmed aerial kills and seven ground victories with the 479th FG, many historians believe that Hollingsworth enjoyed considerably more success. However, he loathed filing combat reports, and duly missed out on being officially recognised as an ace (*Tom Hollingsworth*)

48th FS pilots Bill Broome, Herbert Ross, Fred Haupt and John Lindstrom pose with Bob Hope in front of Ross's *2nd LITTLE KARL* at Saint Marie du Zit in July 1943. Hope was on one of his famed USO trips entertaining the troops, whilst the 48th FS was just beginning to build its incredible scoring record of 159 confirmed kills – the highest tally in the 14th FG. Herbert Ross was later nicknamed 'Herbie the Boat Sinker' following his precision attack on the famous pre-war Italian ocean liner *Rex*, which saw him put a bomb down one of the vessel's funnels (*Weatherford*)

would also later achieve 'ace status' flying P-38s in England, this time with the P-38J-equipped (later exchanged for P-51Ds, a type Johnson used to claim his sixth and seventh victories on 11 September, and in which he was later shot down and killed on the 23rd of the same month) 479th FG – indeed his fifth kill, scored on 22 June 1944, was also his unit's first confirmed victory. Fellow 82nd FG pilot Louis Curdes got his final two victories (Bf 109s) on 27 August in P-38G-10 42-13150, thus raising his tally to eight. The pilot then suffered mechanical trouble which forced him down near Benevento, where he was duly captured. Curdes remained in captivity for a only a matter of days, however, as he and several other P-38 pilots managed to effect an escape and subsequently survive behind enemy lines until crossing into Allied territory on

P-38F-1 41-7649 "WALLY" was used by 48th FS CO, Maj W C Walles, in late 1942. It is seen here just moments after take-off from Youks-les-Bains airfield, in Algeria (Jerry Scutts)

Lt Sidney Weatherford of the 48th FS admires the markings on his P-38G. The phrase TOMMIE'S LUCKY PENNY was a promise the pilot had made to his wife that he would turn up again after his combat days had ended – he scored five victories before he made good his promise. Sadly, flame-haired Sidney Weatherford was killed in action near Wonson, Korea, on 11 August 1952 whilst at the controls of an F-84D from the 58th Fighter-Bomber Group (Weatherford)

27 May 1944. Curdes later added a ninth kill to his tally on 7 February 1945 whilst flying P-51Ds with the 3rd FG in the Pacific.

On 2 September Clarence Johnson 'bagged' a Bf 109 destroyed and two probables in what was later described as one of the most intense operations flown by P-38s in the Mediterranean. Charged with escorting B-25s sent to bomb a marshalling yard near Naples, the Lightning pilots encountered a host of enemy fighters as they approached the Italian coast – 23 Messerschmitts were subsequently reported to have been destroyed for the loss of 10 P-38s. Bf 109Gs from JGs 77, 53 and 3 all participated in the engagement, and the *Jagdwaffe* admitted the loss of seven pilots, including 67-kill *Experten* Oberleutnant Franz Schiess, whilst claiming the destruction of 13 P-38s. All the B-25s survived the mission.

One of the most successful operations flown by P-38s in the latter part of 1943 was undertaken by the 37th FS on 9 October. Newly-promoted squadron commander Maj Bill Leverette was leading his unit on a fighter sweep of the Aegean Sea in support of British naval ships when a formation of Ju 87 dive-bombers was sighted about to commence an attack on the vessels. Leverette immediately dove after the diving Stukas in an attempt to intercept them before they could inflict serious damage to the ships below.

During the uneven fight that followed, 16 Ju 87s were claimed destroyed and five classified as damaged or probably destroyed. Bill Leverette was credited with the destruction of no less than seven of the Stukas, and he recounted this stunning action to Eric Hammel for inclusion in the latter's excellent volume, *Aces Against Germany - The American Aces Speak, Volume II* (Presidio Press, 1993);

'Until nearly the end of the first week of October 1943, the 14th FG was mostly flying in support of our troops in Italy. At the time, however, British Prime Minister Winston Churchill had committed a squadron of Royal Navy surface ships and a small contingent of RAF fighters and bombers to harass the large Italian and German force that was occupying

Lt Richard Campbell of Ferriday, Louisiana, saw action with the 37th FS from the end of the North African campaign to the invasion of Italy. He got his first two victories (Bf 109s) on 18 May 1943 whilst escorting B-17s on a raid against the Trapani Milo airfield on Sicily. An MC 202 and a third Bf 109 followed on 15 June and 9 July respectively. Campbell participated in one of the first B-26 raids to Rome ten days later, and 'made ace' with a brace of Bf 109s (plus one damaged) on 28 August. P-38G-15 *EARTHQUAKE McGOON* was his assigned Lightning throughout his tour. Campbell later served on the China-Burma-India front in 1945 (*USAF*)

the Dodecanese Islands, which are in the Aegean Sea off the south-west coast of Turkey. It was Churchill's plan to invade the islands and somehow bring Turkey into the war on our side. Churchill pestered Gen Dwight Eisenhower into providing a force of American fighters for this side-show operation, and the 1st and 14th FGs were selected. On 4 October, we suddenly moved from our more-or-less permanent base at Sainte-Marie-du-Zit, Tunisia – 30 miles south of Tunis – to a crude RAF satellite field known as Gambut-2, near Tobruk, Libya, about eight miles west of the Egyptian border.

'On 9 October, at 1030 hours, I took off with nine P-38s from the 37th FS. We were to cover a force of one Royal Navy cruiser and four Royal Navy destroyers that were bombarding the German and Italian garrison on the Isle of Rhodes. Shortly after take-off, two planes were forced to return to Gambut-2 because of engine trouble. This left me with Red Flight, which consisted of three P-38s. I was leading Red Flight and Lt Wayne Blue was leading White Flight.

This 27th FS/1st FG P-38G was forced to belly-land at the group's Gerbini base, on Sicily, on 6 September 1943 after sustaining combat damage. Two ubiquitous GMC trucks have been rapidly rigged up with lifting hoists in order to remove the forlorn fighter from the middle of the airfield (*Howard Levy via Aeroplane*)

Lts Hattendorf, Walker and Schoenberg of the 97th FS pose beneath squadron 'war horse' P-38F-15 43-2112, nicknamed *"SAD SACK"*. Frustratingly for Jack Walker, he finished his combat tour with four victories and a probable – although comments made by a German ace touring the USA years later tend to indicate that *he* may have been Walker's fifth confirmed victim, as he casually requested to see the P-38 man's flight plan to set the record straight! (*Blake*)

'We flew all the way on the deck to stay beneath the German radar coverage from Crete. We sighted the British warships at almost exactly noon, 15 minutes before we were scheduled to arrive. The ships were approximately 15 miles east of Cape Valoca, on the Isle of Scarpanto (Kárpathos). I contacted them on their radio-control frequency and was told they had *been* attacked. I misunderstood, however, and thought the controller had

The 96th FS's Lt William J 'Dixie' Sloan is seen in front of his P-38G-5 42-12830 *Snooks IV1/2* at the end of his combat tour on 9 August 1943, having accounted for eight German and four Italian aircraft between 7 January and 22 July. He remained the top American ace in the Mediterranean until 1944, and later flew over 50 missions with the redesignated USAF during the Berlin Airlift of 1948 (*National Archives*)

said that the ships were *being* attacked. I could see that the cruiser was smoking from the stern.

'I led my P-38s up to 6000 ft and began a counter-clockwise circle around the ships just out of range of nervous anti-aircraft gunners. As I reached 8000 ft and was about halfway through the first circuit, Lt Homer Sprinkle, the number four man in my flight, called out, "Bogies at one o'clock!" There was a cloud of them in the distance. They were slightly higher and approaching the ships from the north-west.

'I immediately added power to speed up the climb, and I changed course to pass slightly behind the bogies, in order to make a positive identification as to the type of enemy aircraft. It quickly became clear that they

Looking rather pleased with himself at the end of a successful mission, Flt Off Frank Hurlbut of the 96th FS poses in the cockpit of his P-38G in mid-1943. Note the Lightning's unique (at least for a fighter) 'spectacle grip' cantilevered control wheel in the the pilot's right hand (*Blake*)

Wearing distinctive 'BA' unit codes on its radiator housing, this 96th FS P-38G is seen at Lecce, Italy, in late 1943 (*Fred Selle*)

were Junkers Ju 87 gull-winged dive-bombers, probably out of Crete or the airfield at Scarpanto. There were 25 or 30 of them, in three flights.

'Before we could get within firing range of the Stukas several of them made dive-bombing runs on the British warships. At least one hit was scored on a destroyer, which broke in two and sank immediately.

'As we closed on the Stukas – it was about 1215 – I told Lt Blue to hold up his flight momentarily in case there were more enemy aircraft, possibly fighters, following the Stukas. With my flight, I immediately closed on the left rear quarter of the Stuka formation. The obvious plan of attack was to get in close to the Stukas and clobber them with short, accurate bursts from our .50-calibre machine guns.

'Before the Germans knew we were there, I attacked the nearest enemy aeroplane ahead of me. I fired a short burst with the .50s from about 20°. Smoke poured from the left side of the Stuka's engine.

'The Stuka pilots who still had bombs aboard jettisoned them as soon as the shooting started. Several of my pilots also reported later that a number of the Stukas jettisoned their fixed main landing gear as well.

'As soon as I saw the smoke coming from the first Stuka, I broke to my left and attacked a second Stuka from its rear and slightly below. After I fired a short burst from about 200 yards, this aeroplane rolled over and spiralled steeply downward.

'I broke away to the left again and turned back toward the formation of Stukas. As I did, I saw both Stukas that I had already fired on strike the water. Even though each Stuka had a rear gunner armed with twin 7.92 mm machine guns on a flexible mount, I'm sure that neither of the rear gunners had fired at me.

'I attacked a third Stuka from a slight angle off its left rear. I opened fire at this aeroplane just as the rear gunner fired at me. The gunner immediately ceased fire, and I saw the pilot jump out of the aeroplane, although I did not see his parachute open. The gunner did not get out.

'I continued on into the enemy formation and attacked another Stuka – my fourth – from an angle of 30°. I observed cannon and machine-gun fire hit the Stuka's engine, and I saw large pieces of cowling and other parts fly off. The engine immediately began smoking profusely, and the Stuka nosed down.

'I broke away upward and to my left, and then I re-entered the enemy formation. Another Stuka was nearly dead ahead. I opened fire again with my cannon and machine guns from an angle of about 15°. The canopy and various parts of this Stuka flew off, and a large flame shot out of the engine and from along the left wing

Leading USAAF 'ace-in-a-day' Bill Leverette is seen here whilst still a flying cadet in early 1940 (*USAF*)

Now a fully-fledged fighter ace, Bill Leverette poses with fellow 37th FS pilot Bob Margison. The latter was credited with one of the Ju 87s downed during the epic 9 October 1943 mission, and also observed many of the splashes left by Leverette's seven victims after they had hit the sea (*Ethell*)

Lt Harry Hanna was credited with having destroyed five Stukas (and damaged a sixth) during the 9 October mission – these were his only successes in a 50-mission tour. He is seen here after having just been awarded the DFC for his part in the operation. Bill Leverette received the Distinguished Service Cross, the second-highest American military decoration (*USAF*)

Fitted with 360 US gal drop tanks, P-38Gs of the 96th FS undertake bomber escort duty (Blake)

root. The gunner jumped out of the aeroplane as I passed it.

'Continuing into the formation, I approached a sixth Stuka from below and to his left rear, but on a crossing course that would take me over to the right rear, heading slightly away from it. I was closing so fast that the only way to bring my guns to bear was to roll the P-38 tightly left, to an almost inverted attitude. As my guns lined up on the Stuka momentarily, I opened fire at very close range and observed concentrated strikes on the upper right side of the engine. The engine immediately began to smoke, and I broke away slightly to my left. My element leader, Lt Troy Hanna (who claimed five and one damaged during this engagement, Ed.), saw this aeroplane strike the water.

'I attacked the seventh Stuka from straight behind and slightly below. The rear gunner fired at me briefly, but he stopped as soon as as I fired a short burst of my own. As the Stuka nosed slightly down, I closed to minimum range and fired a short burst into the bottom of the engine and fuselage. Some Stukas were known to have wooden propellers, and this one acted as though its prop had been shattered and completely shot away. The Stuka abruptly and uncontrollably pitched downward, and I was instantly looking broadside at a nearly vertical Stuka directly in front of me. I was already committed to passing underneath him, so I intuitively jammed the control yoke forward as hard as I could. I heard and felt a large *thump* as I went past him. Looking back, I saw a falling object that I at first feared was my left tail. But the tail was still in place. The

Although of poor quality, this rare scrapbook photo shows 14th FG CO Col Oliver Taylor's P-38G *PAT II*. The colonel's impressive combat record has been meticulously recorded on the fuselage just forward of the wing root (*Taylor*)

falling object was probably the Stuka pilot or rear gunner, who had been catapulted out of his cockpit by the negative G forces that were exerted on the plunging Stuka.

'After we landed, it became obvious that the jolt I had felt was from my left propeller cutting into the Stuka with almost two feet of all three blades. The damage to the leading edge of the blades was surprisingly light. We later reasoned, in view of the minor damage, that the prop most likely sliced through a light structure, probably the rudder and fin. This indicated that instead of passing underneath the Stuka, as I intended, I had actually grazed across the uppermost section of the steeply diving German aeroplane. Fortunately for me, the Stuka went down faster than my P-38, or I would have ploughed headlong into it.

'By this time, the surviving Stukas were approaching the south coast of the Isle of Rhodes, and all of my pilots had declared themselves out of ammunition. My own guns had all stopped firing – out of ammo – during my last pass. At about 1230, we made a 180° right turn around a lighthouse on a big rock off the southern tip of Rhodes and headed south.

'In addition to my seven kills, Lt Troy Hanna was credited with five Stukas destroyed, Lt Wayne Blue got one aeroplane (a lone Ju 88 twin-engined type that had closely followed the Stukas), Lt Homer Sprinkle (Hanna's wingman) got three Stukas and a Stuka probable, and Lt Robert Margison (Blue's wingman) got one Stuka. That's 16 Stukas and 1 Ju 88.'

German records admit to the loss of eight dive-bombers, but Leverette believes that the total of sixteen is accurate as one of the P-38 pilots descended to the surface of the water to count the splashes left by the downed German aircraft and confirmed that the number was definitely in double digits. Whatever the truth of the matter, Leverette claimed a record number of confirmed kills for a single P-38 flight in the ETO/MTO, and was duly awarded a Distinguished Service Cross.

Maj Warner Gardner (wearing a personalised A-2 jacket adorned with 95th FS patches) is seen conversing with his groundcrew in front of P-38J *"LITTLE BUTCH V"*. Gardner, who gained all five of his victories in June/July 1944, later died on 9 September 1968 as a result of injuries he had suffered in a hyrdoplane accident during a race on Lake Michigan 24 hours earlier (*Blake*)

Lt Franklin Lathrope and Cecil Quesseth are seen in southern Italy in 1944. Lathrope became one of the last aces of the 94th FS when on 10 May 1944 he claimed two Bf 109s to add to his previous trio of Messerschmitt fighters destroyed (*Cook*)

With his P-38J streaming oil (note the black coating beneath the right engine and lower tailpane, and the feathered propeller), the pilot of this 27th FS/1st FG Lightning has decided to formate closely with the 2nd BG B-17Gs below him in order to rely on them for protection in an impromptu exchange of roles (*IWM*)

15TH AIR FORCE

At the beginning of November 1943 all P-38 units were transferred to the newly-organised, and strategic-optimised, Fifteenth Air Force. The record of the P-38 with the Twelfth Air Force was impressive, for in the year of operations from the commencement of the North African campaign to the transfer to the Fifteenth, the P-38 had generated 37 aces who had claimed more enemy aircraft than any other fighter type serving in the USAAF. By comparison, American-flown Spitfire squadrons had generated 12 aces and P-40 units just 10.

Veteran P-38 aces continued to accrue victories with the new Fifteenth too, Bill Leverette, for example, scoring a further four kills starting with a Bf 109 during an escort mission to Athens on 14 December. Paul Wilkins also claimed victories for the 37th FS, downing a Bf 109 on 16 December, an Fw 190 on 10 January 1944 and another Bf 109 three days later.

For 94th FS aces Lts Richard Lee and Donald Kienholz, their tallies straddled the change over. The former pilot added an Fw 190 on 11 November and two Bf 109s on 11 March 1944 to his successes in August and September, whilst Kienholz, having scored in August and October, claimed his fourth (an Fw 190) on 20 December, his fifth (another Fw 190) on 21 January 1944 and his last (a Bf 109) nine days later.

During April 1944 four Fifteenth Air Force groups converted to the P-51B/C, this change marking the start of the gradual decline of the P-38 as the Mustang took the lion's share of the escort missions – and consequently the majority of kills. By March 1945 the 82nd FG's long-standing victory record had been bettered by two Mustang groups, but the P-38 still held a slight advantage in the overall number of accredited kills.

Aerial engagements involving the P-38 had steadily tailed off during

the summer of 1944, and in September no contact reports were filed at all. However, up to that point Lightning pilots had still been undertaking some remarkable missions, producing further aces.

The first of these missions came on 2 April when the 1st, and 82nd FGs escorted B-17s and B-24s sent to bomb the notoriously difficult target of Steyr, in Austria. Eleven victories were recorded for no losses by the pilots of these groups, but the 'star performers' of the day were the men of the 14th FG, who arrived to perform their target support role just in time to intercept 75 Axis fighters hell-bent on attacking the bomber formation. In a savage

action that lasted for 20 minutes, the P-38 pilots beat off repeated attacks and downed 18 enemy fighters without loss in the process. Lt John McGuyrt claimed a Bf 110 and an Re 2001 to add to the two Bf 109s destroyed, and two probables, he had claimed earlier in his tour. He would destroy another Bf 109 18 days later for his final victory.

Twenty-four hours after the epic Steyr mission, Lt Roland Leeman (four destroyed and four damaged) used the 95th FS's venerable P-38F-15 "*SAD SACK*" to claim a Bf 109 kill during an escort to the Budapest area. This was reckoned to be at least the 12th victory attributed to the Lockheed fighter, which had scored its first success as long ago as 7 January 1943! Further victories would follow until the distinguished fighter was retired after suffering flak damage during a bomber escort mission in late May 1944 – 17 months in action was surely a record for any P-38.

Lightning aces continued to score throughout April, the 49th FS's Lt Warren Jones claiming two Bf 109s (out of eight credited to the unit) for his second and third victories during an escort mission to Italian marshalling yards on the 7th, squadronmate, and future ace, Lt Louis Benne also getting a pair of Messerschmitts for his first kills. Bill Leverette scored his 11th victory – a Bf 110 – whilst performing the role of bomber escort five days later, and Lt Tom Maloney went one better with two Bf 110s confirmed protecting bombers sent to Wiener-Neustadt on 23 April. These were his second and third victories. Lt Franklin Lathrope, meanwhile, got his second (of five) Bf 109 during the same 1st FG escort.

May saw some of the 14th FG's wildest ever dogfights, which resulted in several of the group's pilots becoming aces. Lt Jack Lenox had damaged two Bf 109s and probably destroyed another before he finally scored his first confirmed Messerschmitt victory during a 23 May escort to an Italian marshalling yard. Twenty-four hours later Lenox was on another escort – this time to an Austrian airfield – when he shot down an 'Me 210' (most likely an Me 410) and then found himself on the tail of a second enemy fighter whose pilot was trying to abandon his disintegrating aircraft. Fascinated by the scene unfolding in front of him, Lenox stopped

Described as a 'hot and aggressive' pilot by his contemporaries in the 14th FG, Lt Phil Goldstein accounted for eight German aircraft – split evenly between air and ground kills. His strafing successes were never confirmed, however, hence the swastikas *without* circles on his provocatively named P-38. He and fellow Jew Lt Bob Seidman enjoyed taunting the 'master race' with their impudently marked fighters

Lt Seidman claimed three Bf 109s destroyed and another damaged on his first combat in December 1943. Although he later 'made ace' with two more Messerschmitt victories in 1944, Seidman was shot down and killed by flak on 14 May whilst flying P-38J 42-104259 (*Huff*)

'Ace-in-a-day' and Ploesti survivor Lt Herbert 'Stub' Hatch points to the swastikas that denote his victories on the nose of his P-38H *Mon Amy*. After the war it was discovered that the Fw 190s he thought he had shot down on 10 June were in fact Romanian I.A.R.80s (*USAF*)

firing and turned on his gunsight camera. However, a second foe used the P-38 pilot's fixation with his target to slip in and heavily damage the Lightning.

Lenox quickly took evasive action and checked himself, and his aircraft, out once the enemy had been shaken from his tail. His left engine was shot out, but even more serious was the shattered canopy and spatter of blood around the left arm that he could no longer move. Lenox took a pain-killing shot from the hypodermic needle in his emergency pack and set an anxious course for home. Fortunately, the P-38 was still in good flying shape and his paralysed arm had been merely caught on a throttle lock. The blood had come from the smallest scratch, and Lenox was disgusted with himself for the mild panic that had seen him use the hypodermic needle.

Two days later Lenox was flying on the wing of 14th FG Commander, Col O B Taylor, during an escort to French airfields when the latter went into a terminal velocity dive in his P-38J in order to confirm the crash of an Fw 190 for his fifth kill – indeed, this manoeuvre had been so ferocious that the experienced 'Obie' Taylor had difficulty recovering from it. With certain relief he looked around after pulling out of the dive and was surprised to find that Lenox was still alongside him in formation!

Lenox went on to score his final victories on yet another spectacular mission to Petfurdo, Hungary, on 14 June. Although the 49th FS arrived on station late, it nevertheless caught tardy defending fighters scrambling to attack the bombers in a brisk dogfight. Lenox despatched two Bf 109s in flames and sent another down trailing dark smoke – he was later credited with having destroyed all three. Louis Benne also got amongst the enemy whilst leading a flight of relatively inexperienced pilots, 'bagging' two Bf 109s before both the engines in his P-38J-15 (42-104229) were shot out and he was forced to take to his parachute. Later, whilst in a nearby hospital recovering from his wounds, now PoW Benne had the unusual experience of meeting the pilot who had shot him down!

May 1944 was also a notable month for the 14th FG for other reasons too, for the eventual top scoring P-38 ace of the group (and the entire Fifteenth Air Force for that matter) joined the 48th FS on the 17th. Lt Michael Brezas would go on to score 12 kills in seven weeks between 8 July and 25 August – those who knew him claim that his tally was much higher, but the modest Brezas scorned personal glory. Despite his nor-

mally mild manner, Brezas had nothing but scorn for the Soviet forces who treated him so 'uncomradely' after he had been shot down and spent time in their care. He later claimed that his treatment was so bad that he would search the skies for Russian as well as German aircraft!

Two other 49th FS pilots showed a similar disdain for the anti-semitic policies of the Nazi regime. Lt Bob Seidman had a Star of David painted on the nose of his P-38 to challenge thus-minded German pilots, whilst Lt Phil Goldstein went a step further by naming his P-38J-15 *JEWBOY* in both English and German. Seidman got five Bf 109s in the air before being lost to flak during a strafing mission on Udine in P-38J 42-104259 on 14 May. Goldstein claimed an Fw 190 on 25 May for his third, and last, kill, and is also unofficially credited with four ground victories.

P-38J-15 43-28258 *PAT III* is seen being taxied into the 14th FG dispersal at Triolo, Italy, by Col Oliver B 'Obie' Taylor sometime during early June 1944. The colonel contracted polio soon after this shot was taken and he was invalided home (*Taylor*)

'Obie' Taylor and his faithful ground-crew pose for the camera (*Taylor*)

PLOESTI

One of the most daring – if not entirely successful – missions flown by P-38s during the Mediterranean war was the Ploesti raid of 10 June 1944, the 1st and 82nd FGs sending no less than 94 Lightnings to dive-bomb the Romano-Americano refinery with 46 1000-lb bombs. The 1st FG was tasked with providing fighter cover for the operation, which saw the P-38s go in low under enemy radar before climbing to bombing altitude.

Somewhere along the line the 71st FS erred from the flight plan and strayed directly over an enemy airfield. In one fateful moment the Lightning formation divided and shot down a transport aircraft and several fighters, before being bounced by a large formation of Romanian

I.A.R.80 fighters. Lt Herbert 'Stub' Hatch was about to turn to the left with his flight when one of the I.A.R.80s closed on him from the right, allowing the P-38 pilot to simply manoeuvre into the Romanian fighter and shoot it down. As the I.A.R.80 dived earthwards, Hatch now found himself facing at least five more enemy fighters.

Totally outnumbered, Hatch watched the lead element of his flight decimated before he could actually do anything about it. His wingman, Lt Joe Morrison, stayed on Hatch's wing long enough to watch him shoot down two more I.A.R.80s, and probably destroy or damage several others fastened to the tails of other 71st FS P-38s. After claiming two more enemy fighters destroyed and three damaged or destroyed, Hatch ran out of ammunition. The entire combat had taken place at little more than a few hundred feet over a plain between mountains.

Emmit Wilson and Lt Michael Brezas flank the 48th FS's victory scoreboard at Triolo in early August 1944. A quick examination of the latter reveals that Brezas was clearly the most productive pilot in the unit when it came to destroying the enemy – a further two swastikas would have to be squeezed in alongside his name before the month was out (*Collins*)

95th FS squadronmates Maj Warner Gardner and Lt Charles Adams exchange mutual congratulations in the wake of a one-sided action fought over Austria on 8 July 1944. Adams destroyed three Me 410s and Gardner claimed a fourth during the mission, raising the former pilot's tally to six and the latter's to four. Gardner 'made ace' 18 days later when he downed a by now rare He 111 over Manesti airfield (*Blake*)

Charles Adams points to the six swastikas that decorated the nose of his P-38J-15 *Judy Ann* (43-28796). He only used this machine to down one of his victims (a Bf 110 on 26 June) however. The tactical situation on 8 July so favoured the 82nd FG that Adams felt a twinge of conscience in the wake of his trio of victories (*Adams via Blake*)

Most of the 71st FS were shot down (22 P-38s were lost in total) before Hatch's flight could react, and the 'ace-in-a-day' was the only squadron member to reach home after the mission. Several pilots landed at Allied bases, or were forced down between the target and home, whilst a number became PoWs and others (including Joe Morrison) found their way back on foot. Verifying evidence (ciné film and eyewitness accounts) saw Hatch credited with five confirmed, one probable and one damaged.

Everett Miller of the 94th FS also scored his final three kills during the Ploesti mission to be credited with five victories overall. At around midday he had encountered an Fi 156 observation aircraft and two Romanian-operated CR 42 biplanes and duly dispatched them all.

A Fifteenth Air Force P-38 slips in close to offer personal protection to a lone B-17 returning from a raid. Bomber crews regularly expressed their appreciation to escorting P-38 pilots, as often the mere sight of the twin-boom fighter was enought to persuade Luftwaffe interceptors to search for unguarded targets instead (*IWM*)

FINAL MTO P-38 ACES

The 27th FS put up an impressive display from the end of May until the middle of August 1944, claiming 40+ aircraft shot down and producing its final two aces. Tom Maloney claimed a Bf 109 on 31 May as did Lt Phil Tovrea, these successes being the former pilot's fifth victory and the

latter's first. Tovrea quickly caught up with Maloney, however, for he claimed an Fw 190 on 2 July for his fifth victory. Sixteen days later, whilst escorting a raid on the Friedrichschafen jet assembly plant, he downed two Fw 190s and a Bf 109 to take his finsl score to eight.

Tom Maloney was leading a 1st FG formation of 12 P-38s on a dive-bombing mission in support of the invasion of southern France on 15 August when eight Bf 109s jumped the American formation. In the wild fight that ensued, Maloney claimed two fighters to take his score to eight. Four days later he was forced down off the invasion shore during another mission, and whilst walking along the beach to find help he set off a land mine. Badly wounded, Maloney painfully made his way through the marshes that thrive in the area for the next few days until he contacted some French civilians, and finally a Canadian soldier. It took Tom Maloney a full three-and-a-half years of hospital treatment to recover.

The last of the 82nd FG aces can trace their early successes back to the ill-fated Ploesti raids. Lt Walter Carroll of the 96th FS claimed an Me 210 as the first of his eight victories on 10 June, whilst Lt Charles Adams was flying P-38J-15 43-28654 with the 95th FS six days later on an escort mission for B-24s sent to bomb Vienna when he and Lt James Holloway (six kills) were forced to steeply dive after a pair of Fw 190s that had latched onto the tails of other P-38s. Each pilot claimed a fighter, Adams as his second victory and Holloway as his first.

On 26 June the 82nd FG ran into another determined fight when twin-engined Messerschmitt fighters doggedly attacked their bomber formation, losing 12 to the P-38s. Charles Adams, flying his usual P-38J-15 (43-28796), destroyed a Bf 110, James Holloway claimed another

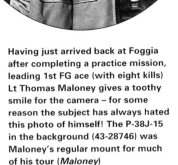

Having just arrived back at Foggia after completing a practice mission, leading 1st FG ace (with eight kills) Lt Thomas Maloney gives a toothy smile for the camera – for some reason the subject has always hated this photo of himself! The P-38J-15 in the background (43-28746) was Maloney's regular mount for much of his tour (*Maloney*)

This P-38L-1 was christened *Maloney's Pony* in September 1944 in the absence of the well-liked ace, who had been grievously wounded on 19 August when he trod on a mine after crash-landing his battle-damaged Lightning north-west of Marseille. Maloney never actually saw this P-38 'in the flesh', but was nevertheless heartened to know that his loyal groundcrew ensured that at least some of his spirit remained in the 27th FS in his absence

Zerstörer, Maj Warner Gardner (soon commander of the 95th FS) downed two others for the first of his five victories and Lt Robert Griffith of the 97th FS added an Me 410 to score the second of his five.

8 July also proved to be a 'stellar' day for the 82nd FG, as its pilots claimed yet more twin-engined fighters. Just the day before the group had begun building on its new record of 500 confirmed aircraft shot down – the first group in Fifteenth Air Force to achieve such a tally – by 'bagging' five Bf 109s. Walter Carroll had claimed one of for his fourth victory, followed by three Me 410s on 8 July. Charles Adams also claimed three Messerschmitt 'twins' on this day to take his tally to six. Years later Adams remembered the mission with a touch of bitter irony – 'I shot them all from behind', he would shrug with a laconic voice. 'Was that fair?'

Whether it was fair or not, the 82nd claimed all 16 fighters encountered in a classic interception. The Me 410s were spotted in clear skies, and the Lightning pilots were duly able to position themselves to cut off any escape. After the mission the interrogating officers had to cut the debriefing short when they received more claims than there were Me 410s in the formation! Sixteen were claimed, with an added three Bf 109s, one Fw 190 and a trainer, for a total of 21 aircraft shot down for no losses. Robert Griffith was credited with one of the Bf 109s for his fifth victory.

On 26 July the 82nd escorted B-24s to the Vienna area in a mission which culminated with the last victories for its aces. Warner Gardner got a He 111 for his fifth kill, Walter Carroll an Fw 190 for his eighth and Maj Claud Ford, CO of the the 97th FS, a Bf 109 for his fifth.

Fittingly, Michael Brezas gained the last confirmed victories for the P-38 aces when he downed two Fw 190s and damaged another during a mission to Czechoslovakia on 25 August 1944. It was appropriate that the last victories scored by a P-38 ace should be credited to the Fifteenth's ranking Lightning pilot, who had gained 12 kills in such a short time. Even though P-38 groups continued to collect odd victories until late April 1945, the days of the aggressive fighter aces were over.

Thomas Maloney shared top scorer status in the 1st FG with fellow 27th FS pilot Lt Phil Tovrea, who claimed a trio of kills to take his tally to eight on 18 July 1944 – Maloney confirmed his eighth on 15 August. The two pilots (who occasionally flew together) shared a mutual respect for each other both as fighter pilots and individuals (*Maloney*)

P-38Js of the 95th FS/82nd FG are seen on a long range sweep of the Italian-Austrian border (*McMonegal via Blake*)

COLOUR PLATES

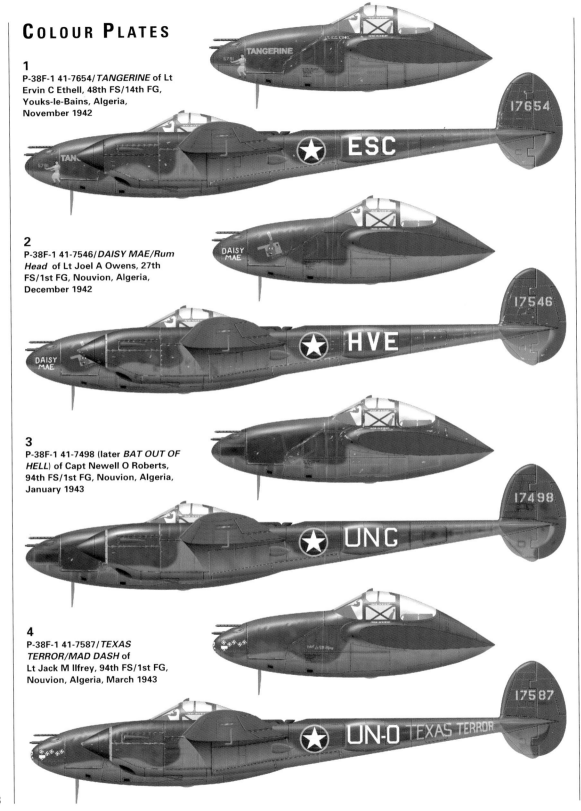

1
P-38F-1 41-7654/*TANGERINE* of Lt
Ervin C Ethell, 48th FS/14th FG,
Youks-le-Bains, Algeria,
November 1942

2
P-38F-1 41-7546/*DAISY MAE/Rum
Head* of Lt Joel A Owens, 27th
FS/1st FG, Nouvion, Algeria,
December 1942

3
P-38F-1 41-7498 (later *BAT OUT OF
HELL*) of Capt Newell O Roberts,
94th FS/1st FG, Nouvion, Algeria,
January 1943

4
P-38F-1 41-7587/*TEXAS
TERROR/MAD DASH* of
Lt Jack M Ilfrey, 94th FS/1st FG,
Nouvion, Algeria, March 1943

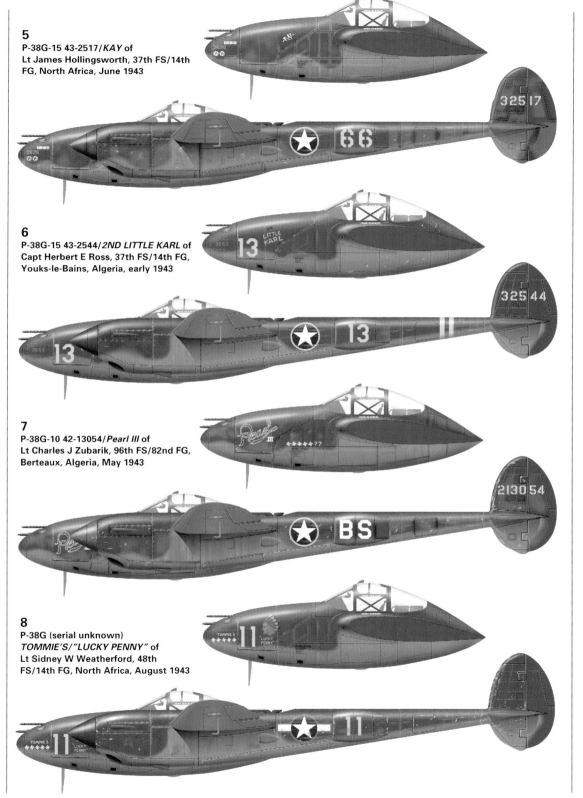

5
P-38G-15 43-2517/*KAY* of
Lt James Hollingsworth, 37th FS/14th
FG, North Africa, June 1943

6
P-38G-15 43-2544/*2ND LITTLE KARL* of
Capt Herbert E Ross, 37th FS/14th FG,
Youks-le-Bains, Algeria, early 1943

7
P-38G-10 42-13054/*Pearl III* of
Lt Charles J Zubarik, 96th FS/82nd FG,
Berteaux, Algeria, May 1943

8
P-38G (serial unknown)
TOMMIE'S/"LUCKY PENNY" of
Lt Sidney W Weatherford, 48th
FS/14th FG, North Africa, August 1943

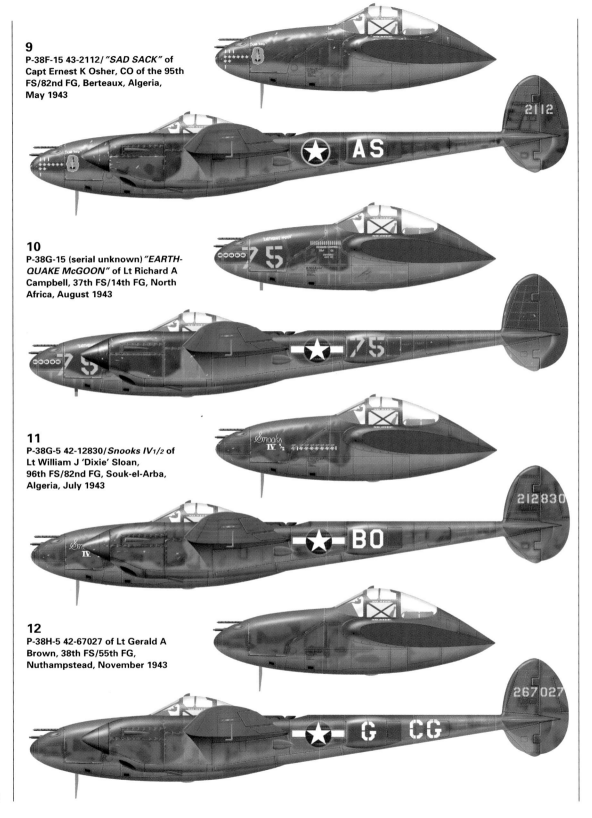

9
P-38F-15 43-2112/*"SAD SACK"* of
Capt Ernest K Osher, CO of the 95th
FS/82nd FG, Berteaux, Algeria,
May 1943

10
P-38G-15 (serial unknown) *"EARTH-
QUAKE McGOON"* of Lt Richard A
Campbell, 37th FS/14th FG, North
Africa, August 1943

11
P-38G-5 42-12830/*Snooks IV*1/2 of
Lt William J 'Dixie' Sloan,
96th FS/82nd FG, Souk-el-Arba,
Algeria, July 1943

12
P-38H-5 42-67027 of Lt Gerald A
Brown, 38th FS/55th FG,
Nuthampstead, November 1943

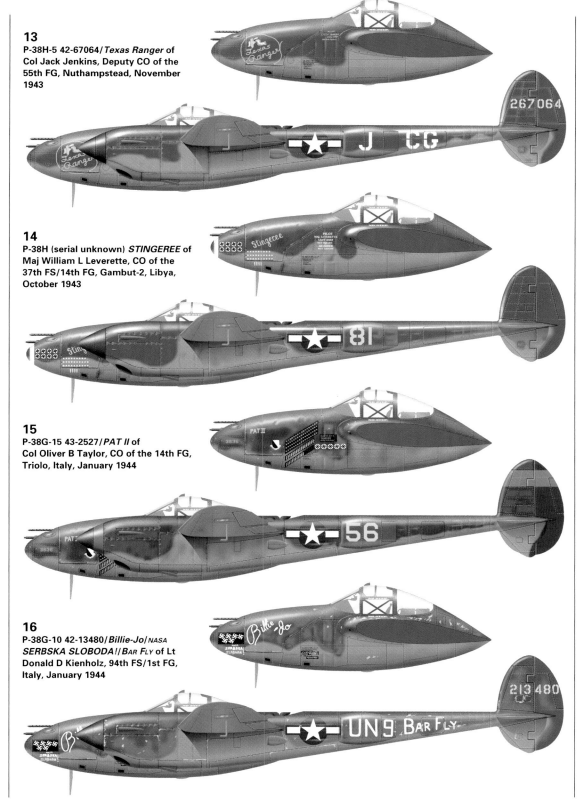

13
P-38H-5 42-67064/*Texas Ranger* of
Col Jack Jenkins, Deputy CO of the
55th FG, Nuthampstead, November
1943

14
P-38H (serial unknown) *STINGEREE* of
Maj William L Leverette, CO of the
37th FS/14th FG, Gambut-2, Libya,
October 1943

15
P-38G-15 43-2527/*PAT II* of
Col Oliver B Taylor, CO of the 14th FG,
Triolo, Italy, January 1944

16
P-38G-10 42-13480/*Billie-Jo*/NASA
SERBSKA SLOBODA!/*BAR FLY* of Lt
Donald D Kienholz, 94th FS/1st FG,
Italy, January 1944

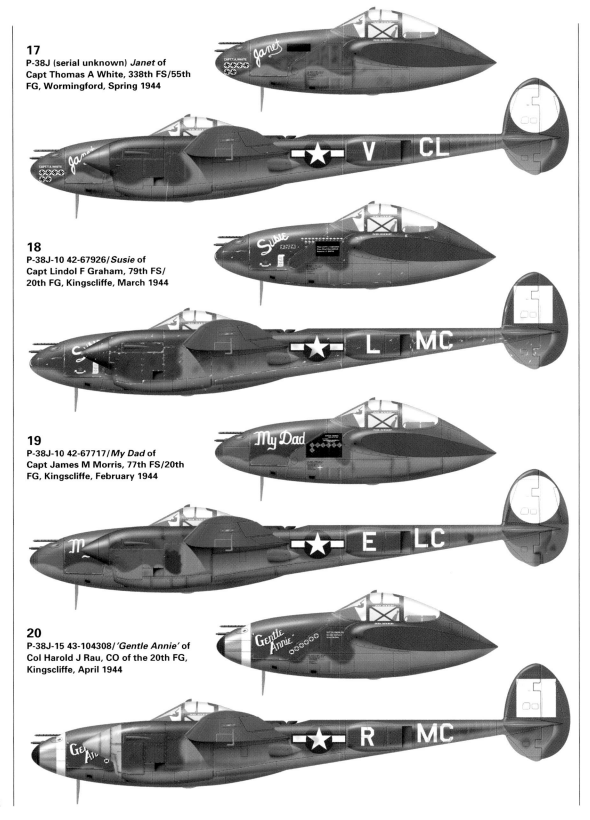

17
P-38J (serial unknown) *Janet* of
Capt Thomas A White, 338th FS/55th
FG, Wormingford, Spring 1944

18
P-38J-10 42-67926/*Susie* of
Capt Lindol F Graham, 79th FS/
20th FG, Kingscliffe, March 1944

19
P-38J-10 42-67717/*My Dad* of
Capt James M Morris, 77th FS/20th
FG, Kingscliffe, February 1944

20
P-38J-15 43-104308/*'Gentle Annie'* of
Col Harold J Rau, CO of the 20th FG,
Kingscliffe, April 1944

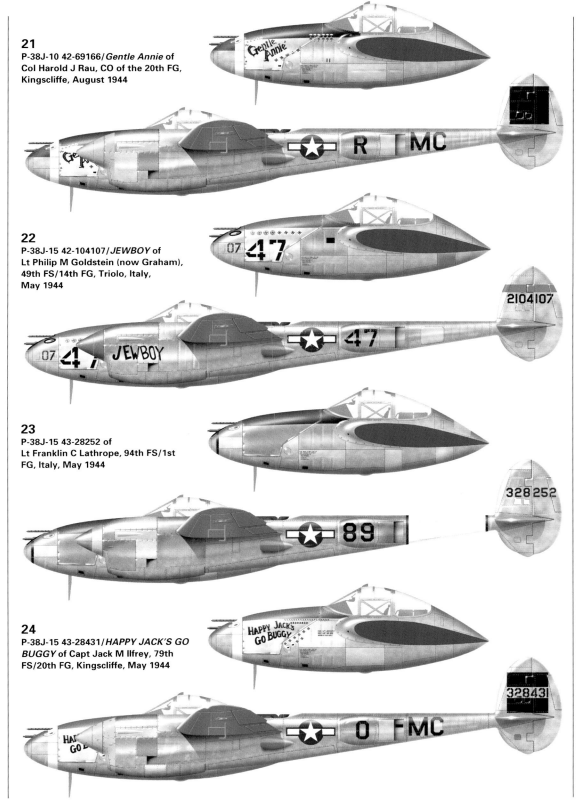

21
P-38J-10 42-69166/*Gentle Annie* of
Col Harold J Rau, CO of the 20th FG,
Kingscliffe, August 1944

22
P-38J-15 42-104107/*JEWBOY* of
Lt Philip M Goldstein (now Graham),
49th FS/14th FG, Triolo, Italy,
May 1944

23
P-38J-15 43-28252 of
Lt Franklin C Lathrope, 94th FS/1st
FG, Italy, May 1944

24
P-38J-15 43-28431/*HAPPY JACK'S GO
BUGGY* of Capt Jack M Ilfrey, 79th
FS/20th FG, Kingscliffe, May 1944

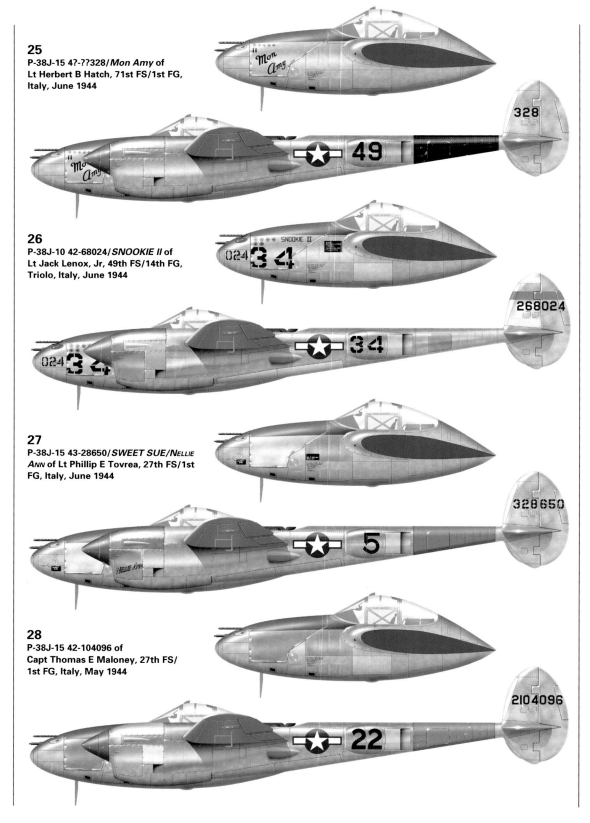

25
P-38J-15 4?-??328/*Mon Amy* of
Lt Herbert B Hatch, 71st FS/1st FG,
Italy, June 1944

26
P-38J-10 42-68024/*SNOOKIE II* of
Lt Jack Lenox, Jr, 49th FS/14th FG,
Triolo, Italy, June 1944

27
P-38J-15 43-28650/*SWEET SUE*/*NELLIE
ANN* of Lt Phillip E Tovrea, 27th FS/1st
FG, Italy, June 1944

28
P-38J-15 42-104096 of
Capt Thomas E Maloney, 27th FS/
1st FG, Italy, May 1944

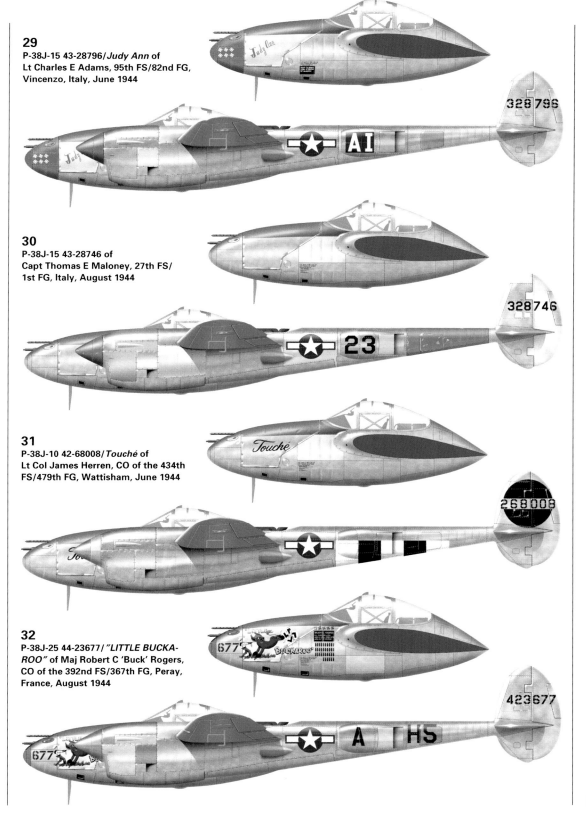

29
P-38J-15 43-28796/*Judy Ann* of
Lt Charles E Adams, 95th FS/82nd FG,
Vincenzo, Italy, June 1944

30
P-38J-15 43-28746 of
Capt Thomas E Maloney, 27th FS/
1st FG, Italy, August 1944

31
P-38J-10 42-68008/*Touché* of
Lt Col James Herren, CO of the 434th
FS/479th FG, Wattisham, June 1944

32
P-38J-25 44-23677/*"LITTLE BUCKA-
ROO"* of Maj Robert C 'Buck' Rogers,
CO of the 392nd FS/367th FG, Peray,
France, August 1944

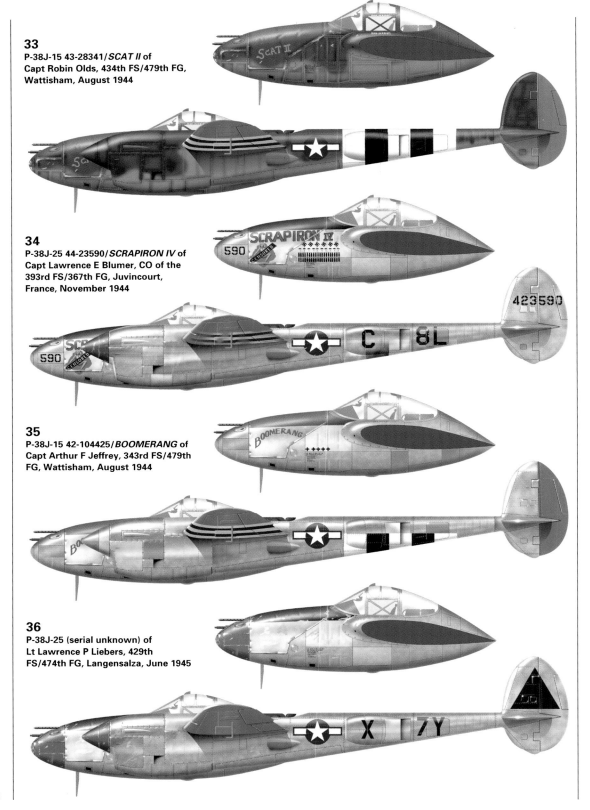

33
P-38J-15 43-28341/*SCAT II* of
Capt Robin Olds, 434th FS/479th FG,
Wattisham, August 1944

34
P-38J-25 44-23590/*SCRAPIRON IV* of
Capt Lawrence E Blumer, CO of the
393rd FS/367th FG, Juvincourt,
France, November 1944

35
P-38J-15 42-104425/*BOOMERANG* of
Capt Arthur F Jeffrey, 343rd FS/479th
FG, Wattisham, August 1944

36
P-38J-25 (serial unknown) of
Lt Lawrence P Liebers, 429th
FS/474th FG, Langensalza, June 1945

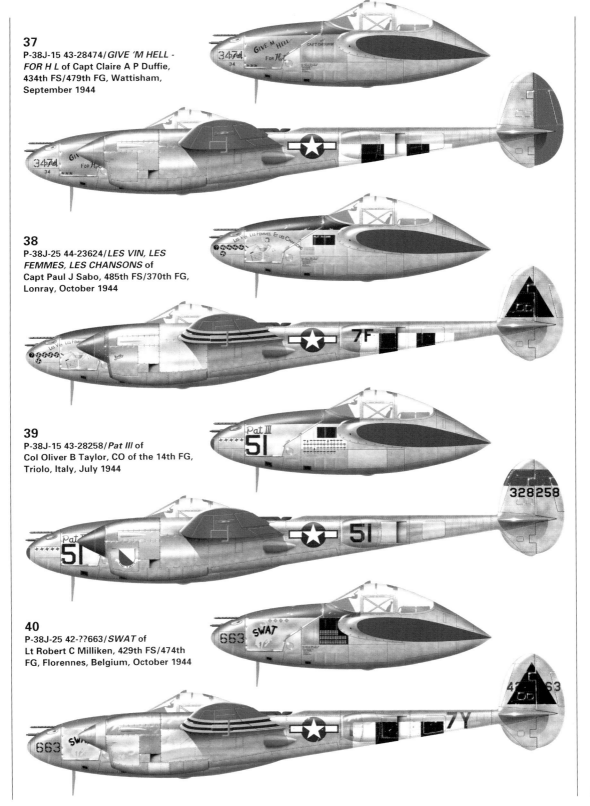

37
P-38J-15 43-28474/*GIVE 'M HELL - FOR H L* of Capt Claire A P Duffie, 434th FS/479th FG, Wattisham, September 1944

38
P-38J-25 44-23624/*LES VIN, LES FEMMES, LES CHANSONS* of Capt Paul J Sabo, 485th FS/370th FG, Lonray, October 1944

39
P-38J-15 43-28258/*Pat III* of Col Oliver B Taylor, CO of the 14th FG, Triolo, Italy, July 1944

40
P-38J-25 42-??663/*SWAT* of Lt Robert C Milliken, 429th FS/474th FG, Florennes, Belgium, October 1944

1
Col Oliver Taylor, CO of the
14th FG, Triolo, Italy, Spring
1944

3
Lt William 'Dixie' Sloan, 96th
FS/82nd FG, Grombalia,
Tunisia, September 1943

2
Lt Richard Campbell, 37th
FS/14th FG, North Africa,
January 1944

6
Lt James Morris, 77th
FS/20th FG, Kingscliffe,
February 1944

4
Lt Claude Kinsey, 96th
FS/82nd FG, North Africa,
March 1943

5
Capt Lindol Graham, 79th
FS/20th FG Kingscliffe,
September 1943

EIGHTH AND NINTH AIR FORCE ACES

When the P-38 returned to combat in England in mid-1943 it was *the* American fighter type of the period – the Thunderbolt still had range, reliability and 'combatability' problems, the Warhawk had proven unsuitable for the ETO and the Merlin Mustang was at least sixth months away from frontline use. Every USAAF fighter group commander wanted the type for his squadrons, but the Lightning was being produced in smaller numbers than any other America fighter, making it the rarest machine of its type on a worldwide scale.

Added to its paucity in numbers was the persistent unreliability of its powerplant – the Allison V-1710 engine – in the cold and damp conditions typically found in north-west Europe. This resulted in large numbers of Lightnings being grounded, thus leaving too few serviceable aircraft available to adequately escort heavy bombers headed for continental Europe on the outward leg of their mission. However, despite being few in number, the P-38's unique planform often alerted enemy interceptors to the fighter's presence, and German pilots would consequently avoid even engaging a single flight of four in accordance with a Luftwaffe high command directive. Consequently, fewer American bombers were attacked and losses became supportable despite the relatively small number of P-38s available.

The Lightning had been reintroduced to the Eighth Air Force in the late summer of 1943, seasoned stateside operators of the P-38 in the shape of the 20th and 55th FGs commencing their work-ups to operational flying in the middle of September. The number of aircraft made available to the newly-arrived groups was barely sufficient to allow operations to commence, the 55th FG having to actually commandeer a number of P-38H-5s from the 20th FG when it flew its first combat sorties on 15 October 1943.

Operations kicked off with a

Lt (later Captain) Robert Buttke of the 343rd FS/55th FG claimed two Bf 109Gs during his first combat on 3 November 1943, a pair of Me 210s and a damaged Bf 110 on 10 February 1944 and another Bf 109G confirmed and a second damaged on 22 April. His final score comprised a half-share in a Ju 88 achieved on 27 February 1945 whilst flying a P-51D (*IWM*)

38th FS pilot Lt Jerry Brown became the 55th FG's premier ace when he claimed a Fw 190 and He 111 on 15 April 1944. he had earlier scored his first victory, on January 31, shooting down a Bf 109G at high altitude (between 28,000 and 33,000 ft) over Venlo, in Holland

sweep over the Dutch coast just 24 hours after the disastrous Schweinfurt Raid, which had seen 60 out of 291 unescorted B-17s shot down and the USAAF's daylight bombing campaign temporarily halted. Stilling themselves for the bombers' return, the Luftwaffe's fighter force left the 55th FG alone as it found its feet in further incursions over occupied Europe. Even the weather was kind to the Lightning pilots, who made the most of clear skies and little opposition to find their feet in the ETO. By November the group was ready to meet the enemy.

On the 3rd of the month the daylight bombing campaign resumed with a raid on Wilhelmshaven, the 'heavies' forming up at about 30,000 ft and being duly escorted for the very first time by P-38s of the 55th FG on the final leg of the route.

Naturally, the Luftwaffe was unaware that the USAAF possessed a fighter that could reach this far into occupied Europe (the P-38 had a range of 850 km, compared with 600 km for the P-51A and 450 km for the P-47C without external tanks), and reacted to the bomber force as it had done in the past. JG 1 sent up a mixed force of Fw 190As and Bf

Capt Chet Patterson of the 338th FS/55th FG was a daring and cunning flight leader who claimed four German aircraft destroyed before being posted home on rotation, having just failed to secure that elusive fifth kill. He was one of the first pilots in the ETO to appreciate the positive fighting points of the P-38 – firepower, range and manoeuvrability (*Patterson*)

Morale remained high in spite of early difficulties with the P-38. These 338th FS pilots watch a colleague demonstrate his rather unorthodox method for combating one of the Lightning's most notorious (and enduring) features in north-west Europe – the icy cold cockpit temperature (*Patterson*)

109Gs to intercept the Americans over Holland. They received a rude surprise.

According to JG 1's records, the P-38 pilots managed to ambush a formation of its fighters and break it up completely. By the time the action had finished, the German fighters had not only failed to inflict significant damage on the bombers, but had themselves been badly mauled instead.

Thirteen fighters were reported lost by JG 1 during this engagement (four Fw 190A-6s and nine Bf 109Gs). P-47 pilots of the 56th, 78th and 4th FGs had accounted for six German fighters, leaving the remaining seven to the 55th. The P-38 pilots claimed to have downed six aircraft, but this number was later reduced to three by the conservative rules of the time. In one of those all too rare moments in aerial combat, it would seem that the 55th FG had actually performed better than it was officially given credit for.

One of the pilots who did receive confirmation for two Bf 109Gs destroyed during this mission later went on to become the first ace of the 343rd FS/55th FG in April 1944. Lt Bob Buttke was a native of California who rose to the rank of captain in the 55th FG, completing two tours (the first in Lightnings and the second in Mustangs) and gaining five victories in P-38s and a 1/2-victory in P-51s. The remaining Messerschmitt downed on 3 November fell to P-38 leader (and future 55th FG CO) Lt Col Jack Jenkins, who also claimed one of the Fw 190s as a probable.

Two days later the 55th FG's 38th FS was escorting B-24s to Munster in rough weather at 17,000 ft when a force of Do 217 bombers, protected by Bf 109Gs (again from JG 1), was intercepted. Once again German unit records indicate that three Messerschmitt fighters were lost in the exchange, whilst all the P-38s subsequently returned to base unscathed.

This level of success was not to last, however, for things started to go wrong as early as the mission to Bremen on 13 November. A savage battle was fought in the thinning air at ceilings in excess of 25,000 ft, which saw the P-38 force reduced to 36 aircraft following the onset of mechanical problems triggered by the cold and damp conditions synonymous with these higher altitudes. Seven P-38s were lost and 16 others badly damaged, with only seven German interceptors being claimed in return. The bomber force took light losses 'on a supportable level'.

One of the damaged Lightnings that returned to its base at Nuthampstead in the wake of the mission attracted both considerable technical interest and sheer wonderment that it had actually returned at all. P-38H-5 42-67027 of the 38th FS (coded 'CG-G') boasted in excess of 100 bullet holes and five cannon shell rips, yet it held together long enough to allow Lt Gerald A Brown – who was to subsequently become the first P-38 ace of the 55th FG on 15 April 1944 – to return to his Hertfordshire base. Much of the damage had been inflicted by a tenacious Bf 109G pilot who had attached himself to Brown's tail and refused to be shaken by the

American's wild evasive manoeuvres. Brown's flight leader, Capt Joe Myers, eventually came to the rescue just as the German delivered a stunning blow that drew plumes of brown smoke from one engine. Fortunately Myers was able to shoot the determined foe down, and thus claim the first of his four-and-a-half aerial victories.

The mission of 25 November was marginally more successful, despite elements of the 55th FG being bounced at 15,000 ft by Fw 190As of II./JG 26 over Lille-Hazebrouck. Capt Chet Patterson of the 338th FS swiftly led his middle flight up to 17,000 ft before diving down to aid another P-38 he had spotted duelling with two Fw 190s. Patterson set his combat flaps for manoeuvre and opened fire at one of the Focke-Wulfs at 300 yards – his wingman saw the fighter catch fire and the pilot bale out.

Four Fw 190s were claimed during the action for the loss of Lt Manuel Aldecoa. After the war it was determined that Knight's Cross holder, and *Gruppenkommandeur* of II./JG 26, Major Johannes Seifert (an *Experten* with 57 kills – see *Aircraft of the Aces 9 - Focke-Wulf Fw 190 Aces of the Western Front* for more details) was killed after his starboard wing had struck Aldecoa's Lightning. The American pilot was seen to bale out, but he apparently died during the descent.

Members of the 20th FG also began flying missions in November in preparation for their operational debut the following month. One such individual was future seven-kill ace Lt James 'Slick' Morris of the 77th FS, who saw his first action on the 29th when he led the second element of a four-ship flight that was operating with another identical formation to create an eight-aircraft squadron.

About 15 miles west of Bremen two Bf 109Gs made a feigning attack from the front that forced the eight P-38s to drop their external fuel tanks.

Capt Lindol Graham and his crew pose in front of his P-38J-10 in late February/early March 1944. Graham named each of his Lightnings *Susie*, and usually flew with the code letters 'MC-L' applied to the fighter's twin booms. His first aircraft was paid for by Lockheed employees and was dedicated to a former worker who had been killed in action. When Graham confirmed his fifth victory his P-38J-10 (42-67926) was decorated with an ace of spades marking, which is just visible immediately above the nose-gear leg in this photograph (*Cook*)

Lt James Morris and his crew chief pose by P-38J *Black Barney* of 20th FG CO, Col B M Russell, soon after the former's record mission of 8 February 1944. Morris claimed two Fw 190s and two Bf 109Gs during sortie in question (*IWM*)

Carrying near-mandatory belly tanks on their inner wing pylons, a flight of 20th FG P-38Hs taxy out from their dispersal at Kingscliffe, Northamptonshire, at the start of another long escort mission in late 1943

The leader of Morris's flight then took off after the lead Messerschmitt, and Morris followed behind to take his turn at the enemy. Under orders to maintain contact with the bombers, Morris stayed with the Bf 109 long enough to fire a burst at the retreating German, but the Luftwaffe had won the skirmish by persuading the P-38 pilots to lose their drop tanks.

Fortunes for the rest of the Lightning escort were not much better, Chet Patterson describing the action as '. . . an all-out, wild, movie style combat spectacular'. He managed to claim another Bf 109 that was on the tail of a P-38, and gave the unorthodox order for his flight to break up and fight individually. That daring command must have worked for all four Lightnings returned home.

The other flights of P-38s were not so lucky, however, as once again seven fighters were posted as missing and still others returned with serious battle damage. Only three Luftwaffe fighters were claimed, but the P-38s had again sufficiently divided the attention of the German interceptors to keep bomber losses down. The month of November came to a close with the P-38 groups having lost 17 of their number, while officially claiming 23 enemy aircraft destroyed.

P-38J-10 42-67757 of the 38th FS/55th FG was the subject of an extensive recognition photo-shoot soon after its arrival in the UK at the end of 1943. The results of the flight were widely circulated throughout Allied air and ground forces in order to familiarise 'the troops' (particularly bomber gunners and AA battery crews) with the shape of the Lightning from all possible angles (*AWM*)

20th FG

By late December 1943 the 20th FG at last achieved operational status. Enough P-38s (including a few brand new J-models) had been received, and a number of pilots had completed missions with the 55th FG. Independent group operations commenced on 28 December with a sweep of Holland by 38 Lightnings, followed two days later by a bomber escort mission to Ludwigshafen, with the 20th providing withdrawal support.

Future 5.5-kill ace Lt Lindol Graham received his baptism of fire on the last day of 1943 when the 20th FG flew a target umbrella mission to the Bordeaux area. Flying P-38J-10 42-67497, he was leading the 79th FS contingent in 'White Flight' as it orbited at 22,000 ft when two Fw 190s were sighted below. He immediately went to 'punch off' his drop tanks in order to configure the fighter for combat, but these would not release for some reason – he was still able to dive after one of the enemy fighters using his combat flaps, however. Before the Fw 190 was able to reach the safety of cloud cover, Graham fired a long burst from 350 yards that produced visible strikes on the fighter's right wing. Although later only credited with having damaged the Fw 190, he had nevertheless commenced his short, but effective, career against the Luftwaffe.

January and February 1944 were good months for the 20th FG. Even though losses continued to be high, the group scored its first victory on 7 January when Lt Willis Taylor claimed a Bf 109 that was about to fire rockets into a bomber formation. The 20th had one of its best days with

20th FG CO Col Harold J Rau is seen with his crew, TSgt James A Douglas, Sgt Grant L Beach and SSgt Luther W Ghent, in front of their P-38J-15 43-104308 *'Gentle Annie'* at Kingscliffe in April 1944. Sitting obediently at Col Rau's feet is his dog Honey (*Ilfrey*)

Jerry Brown and the 55th FG's intelligence officer pose for a publicity shot soon after the former was credited with scoring his fifth victory on 15 April 1944. The P-38J in background was a new arrival for the 38th FS, the fighter being delivered in protective brown camouflage – the 55th FG was by this time flying natural metal P-38s only (*Brown*)

On 21 May 1944 338th FS pilot Lt Peter Dempsey was flying P-38J-10 42-67440 'CL-J' on a bomber escort mission when he went down with his flight to strafe a German airfield on his way home. Spotting telegraph wires in his path a split second before he hit them, the pilot frantically attempted to dive *underneath* them, but only succeeded in getting steel cabling wrapped tight around the right rudder, and chopping the top off the left one! Despite having effectively locked up both rudders, suffered serious flak and machine gun damage and had an engine all but knocked out (which had deposited oil all over his windscreen), Dempsey managed to nurse his ailing fighter back to his Wormingford base (*Patterson*)

the P-38 13 days later when 10 Luftwaffe fighters were claimed during a target support mission for the largest bomber operation flown to date.

Lindol Graham was the star of the day, getting one Fw 190 on the way in, and a further two on the way out. All three aircraft had been zeroing in on the tail box of bombers when Graham had successfully latched onto their tails and caused them to explode. Equally as remarkable as the triple haul itself was the fact that Graham had used just a miserly 583 rounds of .50-calibre ammunition and 36 rounds of 20 mm cannon shell.

Further success came the way of the 20th FG on 8 February when the group escorted B-17s to the Frankfurt area, although the mission did not get off to a good start when no fewer than 14 P-38s had to abort due to mechanical difficulties. James 'Slick' Morris (in P-38J-10 42-67871) was covering one of the ailing P-38s when he sighted a Bf 109 at 12,000 ft. He

67

Inevitably housed in a Nissin hut, the operations room of the 383rd FS/364th FG at Honington is seen after the mission brief on 20 April 1944. The chalkboard at the extreme right of the photo makes the sobering announcement concerning the day's target (*USAF*)

closed in and fired from 100 yards, and the pilot was observed to bale out.

A few minutes later he spotted two Fw 190s taking off from an airfield in Sedan and he duly used his speed and height advantage to quickly despatch both. Morris's flight had by now disappeared, so he wisely decided to set a safe course for home. However, no sooner had he turned west when he came across yet another Bf 109 near the French town of Denain. Quickly latching onto the fighter's tail, Morris scored strikes on the enemy's canopy, but local flak batteries had by now got a track on the Lightning and the American had to be content with leaving his victim heading for the ground pouring smoke at less than 300 ft. Four victories in a single mission was a record for VIIIth Fighter Command in February 1944.

The New Year brought the 55th FG mixed success. There were no great missions in terms of aircraft destroyed, and their loss rate tended to be the highest for any American type during the first part of 1944. The two most destructive elements for the P-38 in northern Europe were enemy fighter action and the weather, the latter not only inducing mechanical failure but also sapping pilot morale with its numbing cold and damp conditions.

However, there were victories to be had in the cold, thin, atmosphere for determined 55th FG pilots. The 38th FS's Lt Jerry Brown overcame these obstacles on 31 January to down his first confirmed victory (he had damaged a *Gustav* near Bremen in P-38H-5 42-67028 on 13 November 1943) near Venlo. He had intercepted a Bf 109G at 28,000 ft and fired at it with his guns until the fighter disintegrated, as his combat report recounts;

'I was flying Swindle Yellow Three on a sweep to protect dive-bombing by another group when, near the vicinity of Venlo, we were bounced by 15

This 77th FS/20th FG P-38J-10 came to grief at the 364th FG's Honington base on 4 May 1944, the fighter appearing to have suffered a collapsed right undercarriage leg whilst taxying for to take-off. The base's fire tenders have liberally sprayed the ground around the rather embarrassed looking Lightning in order to disperse the spilled fuel from the ruptured right drop tank (*Scutts*)

to 20 enemy aircraft from 5000 ft above. We immediately turned into them and started climbing. The enemy aircraft retained their altitude all the time, and would not let us get above them. My flight, led by Capt (Joseph) Myers (4.5 destroyed and 2 damaged), climbed to 33,000 ft trying to get above, and, although we were holding our own, we could not get above owing to their initial advantage in altitude. Because of this, we broke off and started down to rejoin the rest of the squadron. The enemy aircraft half-rolled and came after us. My wingman, Lt Patterson, was bounced and I called for him to break left. The enemy aircraft followed him and got strikes on his right wing. Calling Capt Myers to cover me, I broke down and got on the tail of the '109. My first burst from 100 yards at 28,000 ft hit him on the right side of the canopy. He immediately half rolled and started down, but I half rolled also and closed to 50 yards and

Maj John Lowell of the 384th FS/364th FG is seen receiving his DFC from group CO, Lt Col Ray Osborn, at Honnington. Lowell destroyed or damaged four enemy fighters on his first two missions – 6/8 March 1944. By the time the 364th converted to P-51Ds in late July 1944, he had three confirmed aerial victories and two ground kills. Lowell added a further 3.5 aerial kills to his tally flying the Mustang (*USAF*)

The 55th FG's Lt Marvin Glasgow (extreme left) scored a probable kill and a damaged while flying this P-38J. He is seen here on 11 May 1944 with his groundcrew at the group's Wormingford base (*USAF*)

observed strikes all over the plane. His empennage blew off, as did his right wing tip. After breaking away, I saw the Me 109 going down and out of control. As a result, I claim one Me 109G destroyed.'

On 10 February the 343rd FS's Bob Buttke teamed up with Capt Paul Hoeper when German twin-engined fighters attempted to threaten the bombers on the way to Brunswick. Hoeper was credited with one Me 210 while Buttke got two others (flying P-38H-5 42-67047) and damaged a Bf 110, although he was obliged to come home on one engine.

Following his quartet of kills on 8 February, Jim Morris had to wait just 72 hours to score that all important fifth victory (again flying 42-67871), and thus become the the Eighth Air Force's first P-38 ace. His combat report detailing this historic action read as follows;

'I was leading Blue Flight (77th) Squadron. Rendezvoused with bombers and took up rear position with Yellow Flight on starboard side of bombers . . . Four (4) Me 109s bounced Yellow flight. (We dropped our) tanks and turned with combat flaps into (the enemy). Fired (at the enemy) as Me 109s closed on Yellow Four . . . fired approximately 400 rounds at 60° deflection . . . Saw strikes on E/A and smoke and flame. I then saw it go into an inverted spin. I watched it spin into (the undercast) still in flames at 16,000 ft.'

Although Morris had achieved personal success, it had come at a high price – eight P-38s failed to return to base at the end of the sortie, the 20th FG having claimed just three German aircraft shot down in return during the fierce engagement. These raw statistics prove that the Luftwaffe's favoured tactic of continually battering larger P-38 formations with small, highly mobile, flights of interceptors was proving most effective.

Lindol Graham joined Jim Morris as an ace 12 days later when he claimed two Bf 110s over the Brunswick/Gotha area. This time the 20th FG had a more favourable return, downing five Fw 190s and a Bf 109G, in addition to Graham's pair, for just one loss. On 24 February 'Slick' Morris once again regained ranking P-38 ace status when he downed a Bf 110 over Schweinfurt for his sixth victory.

364th FG

Eighth Air Force bombers began to appear over Berlin in daylight during early March 1944 just as the third P-38 group in the command was declared operational The 364th FG flew its first sorties on the 3rd, and scored its premier victories over the following few days.

Capt George Ceullers of the 383rd FS/364th FG is seen with his men in front of P-38J 42-68017 *Connie & Butch Jnr.* in the late spring of 1944. The pilot used this machine to score 1.5 kills and one damaged in March/April 1944, before going on to claim a further nine aerial victories flying the P-51D (*Scutts*)

On 6/8 March P-38s were credited with just 10 confirmed destroyed out of a total haul of roughly 160 enemy fighters claimed by USAAF fighter escorts. Despite the poor return, three of the victories were nevertheless scored by future 364th FG ace Capt John Lowell. Having previously served as a project officer on the P-38 programme at Wright-Patterson Field prior to his frontline posting, Lowell enjoyed an intimate understanding of the Lightning's capabilities. He first proved his prowess on the 6th when he claimed two Bf 109s destroyed west of Hannover, although one of these was reduced to a probable due to the blurred nature of his gun camera footage – the device had vibrated badly when the quartet of .50-calibre guns housed just above it had been fired.

Two days later Lowell did indeed manage to get two Bf 109Gs confirmed as destroyed north-east of the German capitol. By 9 April Lowell's three aerial victories had been combined with an Fw 190 and Ju 52/3m destroyed on the ground to earn him five credits (and ace status) according to the rules then observed by the Eighth Air Force.

Capt George Ceullers of the 383nd FS also scored his first victories in a Lightning on the 8th, downing an Fw 190 and damaging a second over Berlin – he would later accrue a further nine kills whilst flying the P-51D.

Luftwaffe awareness of the growing escort menace during the first months of 1944 urged more desperation on their part in combating the daylight missions. During the March-April period USAAF pilots noted that German opposition had became notably more determined, and as a consequence greater claims were made by both sides. Record numbers of

Maj Joseph B McManus served as CO of the 383rd FS during the spring and summer of 1944, during which time he completed a large number of bomber escort sorties – just look at the impressive mission tally which adorns the side of his P-38J, christened *Marie*. This photograph was taken at Honington on 15 June 1944 (*USAF*)

Tension or relief shows on Capt Jack Ilfrey's face, depending on whether the mission is beginning or ending. A veteran ace of Operation *Torch* with the 94th FS/1st FG in 1942/43, Illfrey was posted to England for his second tour in April 1944, joining the 79th FS/20th FG. He served as Operations Officer with the unit from June to September, before assuming command of the 79th FS – a position he held until December, when his tour expired. Illfrey had arrived in the ETO with 5.5 kills to his name, and he added a further two to this tally on 24 May 1944 when he downed a pair of Bf 109Gs over Eberswalde whilst flying this very P-38J-15 (43-28431) (*Ilfrey*)

This official photograph shows the first P-38J to land in France following Operation *Overlord*, the aircraft hailing from the 367th FG. This group moved from its base at Ibsley to Beuzeville on 22 July 1944, becoming the first Ninth Air Force P-38 outfit to do so – the 370th FG followed two days later, and the 474th FG on 6 August (*Scutts*)

victories were registered almost weekly by Eighth Air Force fighters as the Luftwaffe lost irreplaceable fighter veterans.

One such desperate mission was flown on 18 March when a mammoth force of more than 700 B-17s and B-24s met savage resistance on their way out of the target area. The standard Luftwaffe policy of avoiding escort fighters was forgotten as the Bf 109Gs and Fw 190s attacked at every opportunity. The 38th FS's Jerry Brown was heavily involved in driving the enemy away from the bombers when he noticed an Fw 190 fastened to the tail of another P-38. He managed to draw a firing pass on the apparently preoccupied German fighter and swiftly shot it down.

Meanwhile North African P-40 veteran Lt Col Mark Hubbard was leading the 20th FG over another part of the continent when he drove his P-38s in too close to the enemy and ultimately paid the price. Although he colonel was not a P-38 enthusiast by any means, he nevertheless wanted the 20th FG to exercise extreme aggression no matter what type aircraft they were using. Leading the group into attack a gaggle of Bf 109Gs, Hubbard had claimed two-and-a-half fighters shot down (with another probably destroyed) before he himself went down in P-38J-10 42-67708 and was taken prisoner. Ironically, in view of his dislike of the Lightning, Hubbard had became an ace during the course of this mission as he had previously scored four kills in P-40.

The 77th FS ran into Bf 110s on 18 March and shot down three of them. These victories were not without cost, however, as P-38 ace Capt Lindol Graham was killed in action. He and his wingman, Lt Art Heiden, were hard on the tail of an evading *Zerstörer* when the pilot put his twin-engined fighter down in the snow. Heiden then watched in disbelief as Graham made a pass at the fleeing German crew, misjudged his altitude and clipped the snow-covered ground, before turning over and crashing.

During the spring of 1944 the Luftwaffe lost all parity with the Allied air forces. Following the 'Big Week' raids on the German aircraft industry, and the Berlin missions in March, the Luftwaffe found itself hard-pressed to counter the aerial threat. With fewer targets to shoot down, the Eighth Air Force accelerated its offensive by attacking aircraft on the ground. Results were initially modest, but by war's end USAAF fighters were claiming more victories on the ground than in the air.

Following the loss of Mark Hubbard on the 18th, command of the 20th FG passed to Lt Col Harold Rau, who led the group with more affection for the P-38, whilst still showing determination to get at the enemy.

On 8 April the 20th FG was scrubbed from an escort mission to Germany because of poor weather blanketing Kingscliffe, but by noon the sky had cleared sufficiently enough for Lt Col Rau to obtain permission for a free sweep to the Salzwedel area. Leading the group at the head of the 79th FS, Rau took his flight through four passes at an airfield north of Salzwedel and claimed 13 single- and twin-engined types destroyed and one 'twin' damaged. Rau himself had got four multi-engined aircraft before seven Bf 109Gs bounced the squadron and shot down a single P-38. Spotting a second Lightning in grave trouble with a Messerschmitt closing in from behind, Rau swiftly centred the German fighter in his

Jack Ilfrey's P-38J-15 (43-28431) draws a crowd upon its recovery back at Kingscliffe following the ace's double Bf 109G haul on 24 May 1944. A close examination of the aircraft's starboard wingtip reveals collision damage sustained during Ilfrey's ramming attack on one of the Messerschmitt fighters during the engagement. This P-38 was later lost on 13 June when Ilfrey was shot down by flak during a strafing run near Angers (*Ilfrey*)

Jack Ilfrey and a groundcrewman make a close examination of the damage for the camera on the afternoon of 24 May 1944. Spares for Lightnings were no longer in short supply by the spring of 1944, and this aircraft would have been quickly patched up with a replacement outer wing section in just a matter of days (Ilfrey)

sights and struck it a mortal blow for his fifth combined victory of the day. Unfortunately the Bf 109G continued on its course long enough to collide with its intended victim, and both aircraft crashed.

Jim Morris added three twin-engined aircraft on the ground (partly shared with two others) to his tally to maintain his position as top P-38 ace of the Eighth, whilst Lt Ernest Fiebelkorn also claimed an unidentified twin-engined machine on the ground to begin a scoring run that would include 9.5 air victories (9 with the P-51D) and two ground kills.

Newly-promoted Capt Jerry Brown also scored on the 8th when he downed a Bf 109G for his third victory. Exactly a week later he destroyed a Fw 190 and a He 111 to 'make ace'. On 22 April Robert Buttke was credited with a Bf 109G shot down and another damaged to also become a P-38 ace – the sole pilot to do so with the Lightning in the 343rd FS.

Despite the fact that the 55th FG would score more than 50 aerial victories during the next few months prior to converting onto Mustang in July, no other P-38 pilot would register his fifth kill.

SUMMER FORTUNES

It was rather ironic that just as the P-38 was about to enter a period much more favourable to securing aerial successes, a decision was made to ter-

One of the USAAF's great fighter aces, Maj J D 'Whispering John' Landers had already 'made ace' on P-40Es in the Pacific as long ago as Boxing Day 1942 when he joined the 38th FS/55th FG in April 1944. He added a further four kills (a Bf 109G on 25 June and three Me 410s on 7 July) and a damaged (another Bf 109G) to his tally whilst flying the P-38J-15, rising to command the 38th FS in early July 1944. Landers' final 4.5 kills were scored with the P-51D whilst on his third combat tour (as CO of the 78th FG) in March 1945 (*Tabatt*)

minate its service with the Eighth Air Force. Warm weather usually brought out the best features in the fighter's mechanical components, and the new J-25 model, fitted with power controls and dive flaps, would largely miss flying with Eighth Air Force groups altogether – although the type served the three Lightning groups within the Ninth Air Force well.

20th FG CO Lt Col Cy Wilson (ex-boss of the 55th FS) was perhaps the only Eighth Air Force pilot to experience success with the modified J-model when he claimed a Bf 109G on 25 June. 20th FG veterans sometimes claim that Wilson was flying a late J- or L-model on this sortie, but he was in fact using P-38J-15 43-28393, with 55th FS codes 'KI-W' – this aircraft was one of about a dozen P-38s that had been modified with kits hurriedly shipped to England. On the engagement in question, the colonel was escorting B-24s out of France when 15 Messerschmitts were sighted below. Wilson gave chase, and his fighter was indicating 450 mph in a near-vertical dive at 17,000 ft when he caught up to one of the Bf 109s and shot it down at 9000 ft.

Eighth Air Force P-38s had one of their best days a few weeks before

Lt George Gleason of the 434th FS/479th FG is seen at Wattisham flanked by his groundcrew early on in his tour in mid-1944. He downed three Bf 109Gs (and damaged a fourth) near Munster on 26 September and also claimed two ground victories with the P-38 – he thought the fighter was ideal for ground attack work, but much preferred the P-51D for aerial combat. Indeed, he scored seven kills with the Mustang after the 479th had traded in its Lightnings in late September (*Gleason*)

Lt Arnold Helding of the 434th FS/474th FG poses with his P-38J, christened *LUCKY LADY*, in mid-1944

converting to Mustangs. On 7 July the 20th and 55th FGs escorted the bombers to oil refineries in Halle, Germany, claiming 25 of the 77 aircraft shot down by USAAF aircraft that day – the 55th 'bagged' 18 of this total for no losses. Incidentally, the group accounted for its 100th aerial success on this date, having commenced operations just nine months earlier. The crack 56th FG (flying P-47s) was the first Eighth Air Force group to break the 100 barrier, doing so in seven months.

The seven remaining victories scored on 7 July fell to the 20th FG, although they lost a single P-38. That latter happened to be none other than the ranking Lightning ace in northern Europe, Capt Jim Morris, who was in the process of shooting down an Me 410 when the fuselage-mounted rear guns of the mortally damaged German aircraft hit his P-38 (J-15 43-28397) and forced the ace to bale out. He spent the rest of the war in a PoW camp, his final tally totalling 7.3 aerial kills and three ground victories.

August was a banner month for all USAAF fighters over the continent, including the P-38s that remained on strength with the new 479th FG (the only Lightnings left within the Eighth Air Force) and the three Lightning units of the Ninth Air Force. There were 27 successful days during the month for fighters of the two air forces, with P-38 pilots not only making claims on eight of those days, but actually dominating the scoring on at least three dates.

One of the most successful Lightning exponents during this period was newly-promoted Capt Robin Olds, who had been flying in the ETO with the 434th FS/479th FG since the group's arrival in-theatre in April/May 1944. A talented and aggressive pilot, whose remarkable leadership skills would see him promoted to command his unit before the end of his tour, Olds finally scored his first kills on the morning of 14 August near Mont-mirail, in France. This successful engagement is recounted in his Form D;

'I was flying Newcross Red Two on a Fighter Rhubarb mission under VIIIth Fighter Command Field Order Number 513. I was alone on the deck heading approximately 330°, when I saw two unidentified aircraft one or two miles away at one o'clock in a turn heading 70° at an altitude of approximately 200 ft. I cut across below them and pulled up behind and identified them positively at Fw 190s. Then I opened fire on the trailing E/A from dead astern, at about 400 yards, and fired a five- to eight-

The irrepressible Robin Olds of the 434th FS/479th FG is seen (with the rank of major) squatting on the wing root of his P-51K 44-72922 *SCAT VI* in April 1945. Eight months earlier he had become the last fighter pilot in the Eighth Air Force to claim five aerial victories with the P-38, adding three Bf 109Gs (downed near Rostock) on 25 August 1944 to a pair of Fw 190s he had claimed 11 days earlier (*Gleason*)

second burst. I observed many strikes on the left wing and the left side of the fuselage, so I changed point of aim slightly to the right and put a concentrated burst into the fuselage. I observed big pieces flying off the German aircraft and wisps of flame and heavy black smoke poured out of it. The E/A then went into (an) uncontrolled half roll going down to the right. At this time we were both just above the trees at an altitude of not more than 100 ft.

'The second E/A broke left in a violent evasive skid right on the deck and I followed, so I did not observe the first German hit the ground because my right wing blanketed him. I was turning inside the second German, so I fired in short busts at a range of approximately 350 to 200 yards, observing a few strikes. The E/A did a complete 360° turn and pulled out straight and level, still on the deck. Then I fired again, approximately a five second burst from dead astern, and observed many strikes. Large pieces of the German ship flew off. He then zoomed and I followed, continuing to fire, still more strikes and pieces occurring. At the top of the zoom the German pilot parachuted, his 'chute opened almost at once, so that I had to cock up on a wing to keep from hitting him. I saw this second German ship hit the ground and explode.'

Olds became the Eighth Air Force's last P-38 ace 11 days later when he claimed a trio of Bf 109Gs over the Baltic coast near the city of Rostock. He would go on to claim a further eight kills flying P-51Ks (see *Aircraft of the Aces 1 - P-51 Mustang Aces of the Eighth Air Force* for more details) by May 1945, before adding a further four MiG victories over Vietnam some 22 years later to raise his tally to 17 destroyed and 1 damaged.

Only one other 479th FG pilot achieved ace status during the group's

P-38 period, Capt Clarence Johnson of the 436th FS scoring his fifth (and the group's first) kill during a strafing mission in the Reims area on 22 June. Having pulled up over a hill in P-38J-15 43-28697 ('9B-R'), the pilot was surprised to see a Fi 156 Storch looming rapidly in his sights. Reacting quickly, Johnson set the defenceless communications aircraft alight with a burst of fire and watched it crash, with the rest of his flight as witnesses. He had previously scored four kills, one probable and one damaged flying with the 96th FS/82nd FG (see chapter three for details) over the Mediterranean during a combat tour completed in late 1943.

The 479th earned a Distinguished Unit Citation for strafing missions in August and September, these sweeps seeing a large number of aircraft destroyed on the ground and at least 25 in the air – a sizeable quantity of ground claims were lodged on 18 August and 5 September, whilst roughly 25 aerial kills were credited to the pilots on 26 and 28 September.

Returning to the 18 August strafing run, passes were made on the airfields at Nancy and Essey which resulted in 434th FS CO Lt Col J M Herren being credited with a Ju 52 and He 111 destroyed, and Robin Olds also claiming a Heinkel bomber and two Ju 88s. Future 12-kill ace (three with the P-38 and nine with the P-51D) Lt George Gleason claimed an Fw 190 and shares in two other machines, whilst Lt Thomas Olson was credited with four aircraft – he followed this success up with two more ground kills on 5 September.

NINTH AIR FORCE P-38s

Three fighter groups within the Ninth Air Force flew the P-38 in the tactical role, the units concerned commencing operations in late April and early May as a precursor for the D-Day invasion on 6 June 1944. Despite relatively few aerial victories being scored by the squadrons within these groups, the 367th and 474th FGs nevertheless managed to generate four aces, plus at least one that completed his scoring in the P-38 after gaining three kills with the P-40 in China – Maj Joseph Griffin shot down a Bf 109 on 17 June and two Fw 190s on 14 August to attain ace status.

Despite having flown operational missions from 25 April onwards, the 474th FG's first aerial kills were not achieved until the afternoon of 6 July when three Fw 190s were downed and a further four recorded as probables. The 429th FS's Lt Robert 'Swat' Milliken was flying P-38J-10 42-67495 during the sortie when he noticed an Fw 190 strafing 428th FS pilot Lt James Frederick as he descended in a parachute. So enraged at the thought of his defenceless comrade being attacked in his 'chute, Milliken dived after the German fighter at full throttle.

The Lightning pilot later recounted how the resulting action was the only classic turning fight he ever experienced in combat. After a few minutes of chasing around the countryside, the Fw 190 was damaged enough to persuade the pilot to take to his own parachute. Curiously enough, the battle had taken place in a wide circle over the same territory, affording the previously defeated Frederick a grandstand view of the action. Once rescued, the downed P-38 pilot could not thank Milliken enough.

25 August was also a day of accelerated aerial combat for the P-38 pilots of the Ninth Air Force, who continued to perform their perilous ground

Robin Olds' squadronmate Capt James M Hollingsworth was as enthusiastic about the P-38 as George Gleason was about the P-51D. Indeed, he used the fighter to claim no fewer than six ground kills in a single sortie on 5 September 1944, which was almost certainly an Eighth Air Force record for the Lightning (*Hollingsworth*)

Capt Lawrence Blumer is presented with the DSC by none other than Maj-Gen Carl A Spaatz, Commander of the USAAF in Great Britain, for his performance on 25 August 1944, when he led the 393rd FS to the rescue of another 367th FG unit that was under attack. Blumer's squadron claimed 14 Fw 190s in the subsequent engagement, five of which fell to the DSC winner himself (*USAF*)

The groundcrewman perched on the wing root of this P-38J seems to be staring at the fighter's complex nose-art rather quizzically. This could be because the aircraft's pilot, Capt Paul J Sabo of the 485th FS/379th FG, was himself unsure as to the number of aircraft he had actually destroyed – hence the question mark on one of the kill symbols instead of a swastika. Sabo, who flew with both the 20th FG and the 370th, claimed a total of 5.333 aircraft damaged or destroyed between 5 February and 20 October 1944 (*Crow*)

attack duties. Undoubtedly the 'star of the day' was the 393rd FS's Capt Larry 'Scrappy' Blumer, who led his flight down behind a gaggle of Fw 190s that were devasting P-38s from another 367th FG unit. Blumer swiftly downed five Focke-Wulf fighters and damaged a sixth, which managed to clear the battle area. Later in the day the 392nd FS made a strafing run on an airfield at Dijon and claimed 16 Ju 52/3ms destroyed, five of these being attributed to squadron CO, Maj Robert 'Buck' Rogers.

The 474th FG also tasted success on the 25th when its trio of squadrons downed 21 aircraft during a large battle in the Laon area – this took the

On 25 August 1944, Maj Robert 'Buck' Rogers led the 392nd FS on an attack on a French airfield in this P-38J-25 (44-23677), destroying five Ju 52/3ms during myriad strafing passes. Unfortunately for Rogers, the Ninth Air Force did not grant credits for ground victories, so the swastikas painted beneath the cockpit of the fighter failed to technically qualify him as an ace (*Crow*)

overall Ninth Air Force P-38 group haul to 41 aerial and 16 ground victories. These impressive tallies came at a price, however, for the 474th lost eleven P-38s and the 367th FG eight. Five-kill ace Lt Lenton Kirkland of the 429th FS accounted for his first two victories – Bf 109Gs – in P-38J-25 44-23565 (coded '7Y-E') on this date.

It was determined after the war that relatively new *Geschwader* JG 6 had lost 16 of its Fw 190s to P-38s on 25 August, thus giving one of the P-38 groups (probably the 367th) a reasonably accurate victory tally.

Ninth Air Force P-38s enjoyed good 'hunting' for the rest of 1944, the 474th, for example, running into German fighters during a strafing mission on 13 October and duly downing 11 of them, with Bob Milliken getting his fourth Fw 190. His 429th FS was in action again eight days later when Lenton Kirkland got an Fw 190 for his third confirmed kill.

November and December were crucial months in the final destruction of the once potent Luftwaffe. Contacts between German fighters and the heavy bombers were sporadic at best, and were in no way threatening the burgeoning daylight campaign. Even the tactical bombing and strafing missions of the Ninth Air Force were now finding more resistance from anti-aircraft fire than from fighter interception.

Not all Luftwaffe fighters had been wiped from the skies, however, as the 367th FG found out on 19 November whilst escorting bomb-laden P-47s of the 368th FG to the Duren area on a ground attack mission – no fewer than 25 Fw 190s were engaged en route to the target. Larry Blumer, who was leading the 393rd FS element of the escort, reacted swiftly to the attack by attempting to drop his tanks but they would not budge. Never-

theless, he still went after the enemy and shot down one of the Fw 190s. He was now one of the elite P-38 pilots to down more than five Focke-Wulf fighters. Other 367th FG pilots claimed six Fw 190s for no losses.

December saw the waning presence of the P-38 in northern Europe, most group commanders within the Ninth Air Force preferring the more rugged P-47 for ground attack missions than the rather delicate (by comparison) P-38. However, Lightning pilots still got in some strikes between the end of the year and spring of 1945, one such December mission seeing the P-38 take a heavy toll of German aircraft when units claimed 19 destroyed in the air on the 17th (on the same day P-47 pilots claimed 55 and P-51D pilots six.) On Christmas Eve Spitfires and Lightnings engaged Fw 190Ds of II./JG 26, and the P-38s claimed two enemy aircraft destroyed and the Spitfires at least one other.

The last P-38 aces to gain all their victories on-type were Bob Milliken and Lenton Kirkland of the 429th FS/474th FG on 18 December. The group encountered about a dozen Bf 109Gs in combat with P-47s northwest of Köln at 12,000 ft, and after shedding their bombs, the Lightning pilots entered the fray. Kirkland got two Messerschmitt fighters and Milliken another to each register their fifth aerial victories.

That was not quite the end of the P-38 aces in Europe, however, for Capt Joseph E Miller, who had scored a quartet of kills with the 48th FS/14th FG over Italy in mid-1943, was transferred to the 429th FS/474th FG in early 1945 to commence a second tour. He duly accounted for a single Fw 190 on 13 March whilst supporting troops pushing into Germany, Miller's victory creating the last P-38 ace in Europe. The Lightning's war in the ETO/MTO had begun in August 1942 with tentative sweeps over France, and did not finally come to end until a 429th FS pilot shot down an Si 204 transport on the last day of the war, 8 May 1945.

Lt Robert Milliken of the 429th FS/474th FG was one of just a handful of P-38 pilots to 'make ace' with the Ninth Air Force. Credited with four Fw 190s and a single Bf 109G between 6 July and 18 December 1944, Milliken also has the distinction of being the last pilot to achieve ace status with the Lightning in northern Europe (*Milliken*)

GROUND CLAIMS

The question of ground claims by USAAF fighter pilots is a troubling one in light of the fact that much of the Luftwaffe was destroyed on the ground during the final phase of the war, with large numbers of enemy aircraft often being rendered useless in a single pass. To make matters worse, the Eighth Air Force was the only organisation to accord ground claims equality with aerial victories in respect to acknowledging the achievements of aces. Recognising that they could no longer compete on an equal footing in the skies during the last months of the war, but still hoping to distract attacks on vital targets, the Luftwaffe lined up large numbers of aircraft at heavily-defended airfields across Germany as a lure for marauding Allied fighters. Although this desperate tactic often saw skilled pilots trained in the art of aerial combat sacrificed in an attempt to destroy mostly non-operational aircraft, American fighter groups took a heavy toll of German aircraft, often claiming hundreds in single sorties.

Heading the strafing tally were the P-51D groups, who claimed over 4000 aircraft destroyed, followed by the P-47 units with 3000+ and finally the P-38 with 749. The paucity of this latter figure reflects the fact that P-38s flew fewer sorties than either the P-51D or the P-47.

Perhaps the first occasion on which the Lightning claimed ground victories was in north-western Africa when the 14th FG destroyed approximately six transports and bombers on the ground (plus a number of others that had succeeded in taking off) on 24 November 1942. The action resulted in several of the participating pilots being credited with at least five combined air and ground victories.

The greatest strafing mission involving P-38s in the MTO was flown on 25 August 1943 when two groups of Lightnings came in 'under the

CRAZY MAIZIE was a P-38H flown by the 96th FS/82nd FG in the Mediterranean in late 1943. Note the mission tally on the extreme nose of the fighter (*Blake*)

Again adorned with a log of completed missions on its nacelle, veteran P-38G *Little Willie* of the 96th FS is seen on a featureless airfield in North Africa in mid-1943 (*Blake*)

radar' and shot up a large percentage of the enemy aircraft found on the various fields scattered across the Foggia plain. Lt Joe Solko of the 82nd FG was flying the unit's celebrated P-38F-15 *"SAD SACK"* on this occasion, and he duly claimed damaging no fewer than nine Ju 88s when he returned to base. Solko had used the P-38's combat flaps to slow the fighter down during his gunnery passes, dropping its nose to a highly advantageous attitude. He later recounted how he practically looked down into the cockpits of the bombers '. . . dancing on their landing gear . . .' as the bullets and shells struck.

In later months, as the Allied armies slowly advance up the Italian peninsula, most enemy aircraft were withdrawn beyond the range of tactical fighters, and fewer claims were subsequently made – far more aerial victories were confirmed on deep penetration missions over defended enemy cities. Fewer claims in general were available to the Fifteenth Air Force, while more ground kills fell to the Eighth and Ninth Air Forces.

Reinforcing the latter statistic, two Eighth Air Force P-38 groups actually earned Distinguished Unit Citations partly because of strafing success. The first citation was won by the 20th FG for a sweep of the Salzwedel area, about 80 miles north-west of Berlin, on 8 April 1944, the group claiming seven aircraft in the air and 21 on the ground.

This mission had only been flown because group CO, Col Harold Rau, had hastily organised a replacement sweep following the scrubbing of a scheduled escort mission due to bad weather. Conditions rapidly improved as the day wore on, and the colonel succeeded in getting permission from Eighth Air Force Headquarters to make the sweep. Forty-four P-38s from the three squadrons duly took off from Kingscliffe at about 1400 hours and arrived over the target a few minutes before 1600.

The Lightnings descended from 7000 ft and generally 'beat up' anything of military value. Rau had already claimed three unidentified twin-engined aircraft and a Ju 52/3m on the ground when he broke off his strafing runs and took his flight back up to 10,000 ft in order to perform

the role of top cover. Although the flak was intense by this time, seven Bf 109Gs made a slashing attack on the P-38s still strafing and succeeded in shooting one down. Rau then attempted to come to the rescue of a second P-38 under attack, and although he succeeded in mortally damaging the Messerschmitt fighter, the German pilot nevertheless collided with the P-38 he was pursuing and both aircraft crashed.

Despite the 20th FG enjoying great success on this day, top honours went to the 479th FG for claiming more than 60 aircraft on the ground (as well as another 29 in the air) during the period 18 August to 28 September 1944. Robin Olds, George Gleason, James Herren and Thomas Olson raised their combined air and ground totals to five or more during this period, whilst James Hollingsworth scored six aircraft (two Do 217s and four Me 410s) on the ground at Ettingshausen, Germany, on 5 September for what is perhaps a record for the P-38 in Europe.

Maj Robert 'Buck' Rogers, CO of the 392nd FS, had his day of strafing aircraft on 25 August 1944, when he led the squadron to an airfield south of Dijon and found it packed with Ju 52/3ms all neatly lined up – USAAF intelligence later concluded that the transports had been assembled to fly important German personnel out of France. All 16 aircraft were destroyed on the ground, and it was determined later by eyewitness account that Rogers had destroyed five aircraft in two passes. Unfortunately for him, there was no provision in Ninth Air Force policy to officially recognise ground claims, so Rogers has only the personal satisfaction of knowing that he destroyed five enemy aircraft.

The matter of official accreditation for aircraft destroyed on the ground is a thorny one. Some pilots of the Eighth Air Force are credited with as many as 10 aircraft destroyed in a single attack, lending credence to the suggestion that destroying grounded machines was a simpler matter than outmanoeuvring an operational aircraft in the air. There is no doubt that special dangers attended attacks on grounded aircraft, but victories were also less complicated by definition of the target(s) being immovable.

P-38Js of the 38th FS/55th FG are seen on a bomber escort mission during May 1944. This month saw Lightnings flying both escort and ground attack missions in preparation for D-Day. Late spring 1944 was also a period of transition for fighters in the ETO, as new aircraft began to be taken on strength in a natural metal finish, rather the traditional olive drab and grey (*USAF*)

APPENDICES

P-38 LIGHTNING ACES OF WORLD WAR 2 IN EUROPE AND THE MEDITERRANEAN

Twelfth Air Force

Name	Group	Aerial Victories
William J Sloan	82nd	12
Frank D Hurlbut	82nd	9
Louis E Curdes	82nd	8 (9)
Claude R Kinsey	82nd	7
Ward A Kuentzel	82nd	7
Lawrence P Liebers	82nd	7
Meldrum L Sears	1st	7
Herbert E Ross	14th	7
Harley C Vaughn	82nd	7
Edward T Waters	82nd	7
Richard A Campbell	14th	6
Ray Crawford	82nd	6
James W Griffiss	1st	6
William J Schildt	82nd	6
Thomas A White	82nd	6
Charles J Zubarik	82nd	6*
Jack M Ilfrey	1st	6** (8)
Paul R Cochran	82nd	5
Rodney W Fisher	1st	5
Harry T Hanna	14th	5
Daniel Kennedy	1st	5
John A Mackay	1st	5
T H McArthur	82nd	5
Ernest K Osher	82nd	5
Joel A Owens	1st	5
Newell O Roberts	1st	5
Gerald L Rounds	82nd	5
Virgil H Smith	14th	5**
Sidney W Weatherford	14th	5.
Darrell G Welch	1st	5
Lee V Wiseman	1st	5
John L. Wolford	1st	5

Fifteenth Air Force

Name	Group	Aerial Victories
Michael Brezas	14th	12
William L Leverette	14th	11
Walter J Carroll	82nd	8
Thomas E Maloney	1st	8
Phillip E Tovrea	1st	8
Charles E Adams	82nd	6
James D Holloway	82nd	6
Donald D Kienholz	1st	6
Armour C Miller	1st	6
Leslie E Anderson	82nd	5
Louis Benne	14th	5
Herbert B Hatch	1st	5
Warren L Jones	14th	5
Carroll S Knott	14th	5
Franklin C Lathrope	1st	5
Richard J Lee	1st	5
Marlow J Leikness	14th	5
Jack Lenox	14th	5
John W McGuyrt	14th	5
Everett Miller	1st	5
Robert K Seidman	14th	5
Oliver B Taylor	14th	5
Herman W Visscher	82nd	5
Paul H Wilkins	14th	5
Max J Wright	14th	5

() Final score in brackets

* Zubarik had two extra victories not officially recognised

** Final scores altered after Twelfth Air Force changed shared victory policy

Eighth and Ninth Air Forces

Name	Group	Aerial Victories
Jack M Ilfrey	20th	8 (scored 6 with Twelfth AF)
James M Morris	20th	7.33
Lawrence E Blumer	367th	6
Lindol F Graham	20th	5.5
Gerald Brown	55th	5
Robert L Buttke	55th	5 (+1 with P-51D)
Clarence O Johnson	479th	5 (4 with 82nd FG, +2 with P-51D)
Lenton F Kirkland	474th	5
Joseph E Miller	474th	5 (4 with 14th FG)
Robert C Milliken	474th	5
Robin Olds	479th	5 (+8 with P-51D and +4 with F-4C with 8th TFW during Vietnam War)

Victory lists of ETO/MTO P-38 aces with 7+ kills

William J Sloan

7/1/43	1 Bf109
30/1/43	1 Bf109
2/2/43	1 Bf109/1 Do 217
15/2/43	1 Bf109
20/5/43	1 Ju 88/1 MC 200
18/6/43	1 MC 200
5/7/43	1 Re 2001/1 Bf 109
10/7/43	1 MC 202

Michael Brezas

8/7/44	1 Bf 109
14/7/44	2 Bf 110/1 Fw 190
19/7/44	1 Fw 190
20/7/44	1 Bf 109
22/7/44	2 Fw 190
7/8/44	2 Bf 109
25/8/44	2 Fw 190
22/7/43	1 Bf 109

William L Leverette

9/10/43	7 Ju 87
14/12/43	1 Bf 109
24/2/44	1 Bf 110
18/3/44	1 Bf 109
12/4/44	1 Bf 110
2/9/43	1 Bf 109

Frank D Hurlbut

11/5/43	1 Ju 52/3m
20/5/43	1 Fw 190
24/5/43	1 MC 202
10/7/43	3 Fw 190
7/8/43	1 Fw 190

Walter J Carroll

10/6/44	1 Bf 109
24/6/44	1 Bf 109
4/7/44	1 Ju 52/3m
7/7/44	1 Bf 109
8/7/44	3 Me 410
26/7/44	1 Fw 190

Louis E Curdes

29/4/43	3 Bf 109
19/5/43	2 Bf 109
24/6/43	1 MC 202
27/8/43	2 Bf 109

Thomas E Maloney

28/3/44	1 Bf 109
23/4/44	2 Bf 110
28/5/44	1 Do 217
31/5/44	1 Bf 109
18/7/44	1 Fw 190
15/8/44	2 Bf 109

Philip E Tovrea

31/5/44	1 Bf 109
10/6/44	1 Bf 109
16/6/44	2 Bf 109
2/7/44	1 Fw 190
18/7/44	2 Fw 190/1 Bf 109

James M Morris

5/2/44	.333 He 111
8/2/44	2 Bf 109/2 Fw 190
11/2/44	1 Bf 109
24 /2/44	1 Bf 110
7/7/44	1 Me 410
5/4/43	2 Ju 52/3m

Claude R Kinsey

29/1/43	1 Bf 109
30/1/43	1 Bf 109
17/2/43	1 Cant Z 506
23/2/43	1 Cant Z 506
15/3/43	1 Bf 109

Ward A Kuentzel

20/3/43	1 Bf 109
20/5/43	1 Bf 109
18/6/43	1 MC 202
28/6/43	1 MC 202
10/7/43	1 Fw 190/1 Ju 88
22/7/43	1 Bf 109

Lawrence P Liebers

14/5/43	1 MC 202
21/5/43	1 MC 202
18/6/43	2 MC 202/1 MC 205
10/7/43	1 Fw 190
20/8/43	1 Fw 190

Herbert E Ross

9/5/43	1 MC 202
18/7/43	2 Ju 52
25/8/43	1 MC 202
26/8/43	1 Bf 109
29/8/43	1 Bf 109
6/9/43	1 Fw 190

Meldrum L Sears

1/1/43	1 Ju 52
12/1/43	1 Fi 156
10 /4/43	4 Ju 52
12/4/43	1 Bf 109

Harley C Vaughan

15 /1/43	1 Bf 109
30/1/43	1 Fw 190
12/3/43	1 Cant Z 1007
20/3/43	1 Ju 88
17/4/43	1 Ju 88
23/4/43	1 Cant Z 501
14 /5/43	1 MC 202

Edward T Waters

12/3/43	1 Cant Z 1007
17/4/43	1 Fiat BR 20
20/5/43	1 Bf 109
18/6/43	1 Bf 109
28/6/43	1 MC 202
30/6/43	1 Fw 190
10/7/43	1 Bf 109

Jack M Ilfrey

29/11/42	.5 Bf 110
2/12/42	2 Bf 109
26/12/42	2 Fw 190
3/3/43	1 Bf 109
8/3/43	.5 Bf 109
24/5/44	2 Bf 109 (scored with Eighth Air Force)

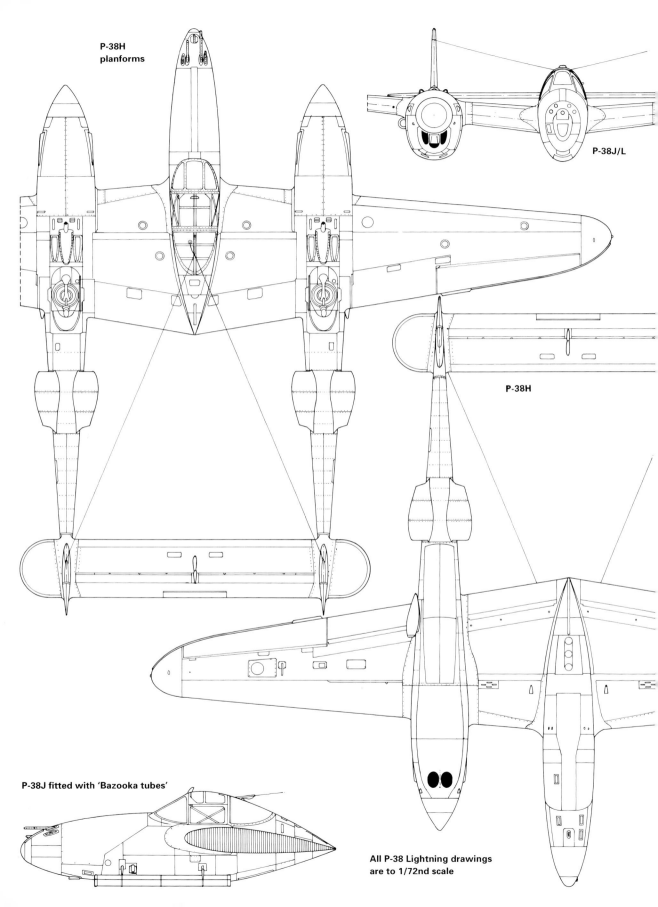

P-38H planforms

P-38J/L

P-38H

P-38J fitted with 'Bazooka tubes'

All P-38 Lightning drawings are to 1/72nd scale

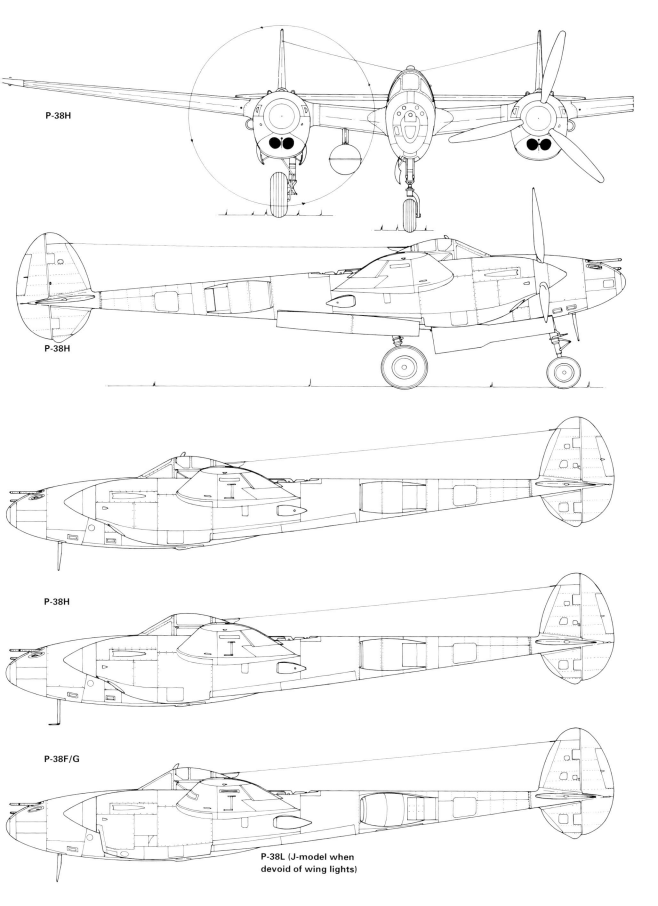

P-38H

P-38H

P-38H

P-38F/G

P-38L (J-model when
devoid of wing lights)

COLOUR PLATES

1
P-38F-1 41-7654/TANGERINE of Lt Ervin C Ethell, 48th FS/14th FG, Youks-le-Bains, Algeria, November 1942

The 14th FG was allocated one of the first blocks of P-38Fs built by Lockheed during the summer of 1942, Lt Ethell flying this example from England to North Africa with the 48th FS in time to play an active part in Operation *Torch*, which commenced at the beginning of November 1942. It did not take the 14th FG long to score its first kills either in the air or on the ground, with several pilots managing to run up combined air and ground tallies before the end of the month. Ethell almost became the first P-38 ace in a single mission when he downed four Ju-52/3ms and a probable Bf 109 on 28 November whilst flying this fighter. He also came close to achieving a record number of ground victories in the P-38, being unofficially credited with ten Axis aircraft destroyed. Unfortunately for Ethell, the Twelfth Air Force only recognised aerial victories, thus leaving him twice deprived of unique records in the P-38. *TANGERINE* was later shot down in action whilst being flown by another 48th FS pilot.

2
P-38F-1 41-7546/DAISY MAE/Rum Head of Lt Joel A Owens, 27th FS/1st FG, Nouvion, Algeria, December 1942

Like Ervin Ethell, Joel Owens also flew his P-38F-1 down to North Africa from England and had begun his scoring run by the end of November. Indeed, he achieved the first kill for the 27th FS, and had scored five confirmed, one probable and a damaged claim by the end of the campaign. The *DAISY MAE* part of the aircraft's nickname was not a reference to the famous cartoon character, but to the girlfriend of Owens's crewchief – the rest of the pilot's flight were not aware of this, and mistakenly adopted names of other characters in the comic strip for their aircraft! *RUMHEAD* is a humourous reference to the state of Oklahoma, the home of several flight members, including Owens. He actually had a star placed on the geographical location of his hometown, Skiatook, on the stylised green map of Oklahoma that adorned the port gun access panel.

3
P-38F-1 41-7498 (later BAT OUT OF HELL) of Capt Newell O Roberts, 94th FS/1st FG, Nouvion, Algeria, January 1943

Roberts used this plain F-1 from the beginning of the North Africa landings, flying it on 29 November when he shared in the destruction of Bf 110 with future ace Jack Ilfrey. Because of the severe shortage of Lightnings, and associated spare parts, in-theatre, some F-1s remained in the frontline long after the North African campaign had ended in May 1943. Indeed, Roberts's P-38 lasted long after he had rotated

home in March 1943, having completed his prerequisite 50 (actually 52 in his case) combat missions. A Lt Hagenback duly inherited the by now well-worn 'UN - G' soon after Roberts left, adding the evocative name *BAT OUT OF HELL*, with appropriately horrific nose art, during the Sicilian campaign in July-August 1943.

4
P-38F-1 41-7587/TEXAS TERROR/MAD DASH of Lt Jack M Ilfrey, 94th FS/1st FG, Nouvion, Algeria, March 1943

Like his contemporaries, Ilfrey flew this fighter from England to north-west Africa, via a temporary stop-over in Portugal due to an engine malfunction. He boldly named the fighter *TEXAS TERROR* on the port boom in order to indicate his predisposition to any Axis airmen he encountered, and *THE MAD DASH* on the starboard boom to commemorate the long overwater flight undertaken by the P-38s to North Africa. This Lightning was damaged beyond repair sometime in late 1942 or early 1943, and was apparently cannibalised to keep other 94th FS P-38s flying.

5
P-38G-15 43-2517/KAY of Lt James Hollingsworth, 37th FS/14th FG, North Africa, June 1943

Hollingsworth was already part of the 37th FS (originally part of the then US-based 55th FG) when it joined the 14th FG in time for the group's second combat tour in May 1943. Although a very successful pilot in combat, Hollingsworth was reputedly so disdainful of combat records that he had to be coaxed on occasion to even mention his exploits. Officially, he is credited with three confirmed aerial victories (Do 217 on 25 May and Bf 109s on 24 June and 19 August 19), one unconfirmed kill (MC 202 on 15 June) and a damaged (Bf 109 on 18 May) during his 1943 combat tour. Hollingsworth later flew with the 434th FS/479th FG, claiming a further seven ground victories.

6
P-38G-15 43-2544/2ND LITTLE KARL of Capt Herbert E Ross, 37th FS/14th FG, Youks-le-Bains, Algeria, early 1943

Herbert Ross scored seven confirmed aerial kills, as well as one probable and a damaged claim, between 9 May and 6 September 1943. There were no traces of victory marks to be found on the photos of *2ND LITTLE KARL* taken during this period, and it is possible that Ross chose not to adorn his aircraft accordingly. The two yellow bands on the aft booms were flight leader's stripes, which suggest that this is how the P-38 appeared during the early stages of Ross's combat tour. The aircraft's nickname referred to the pilot's son.

7
P-38G-10 42-13054/Pearl III of Lt Charles J Zubarik,

96th FS/82nd FG, Berteaux, Algeria, May 1943

'Shorty' Zubarik was element, and sometimes flight, leader of the 96th FS until he was shot down and captured on 24 May 1943 near Vanafiorita airfield. He and fellow squadron ace 'Dixie' Sloan were both element mates and firm friends up until Zubarik's death in September 1979. His official victories included a Ju 52/3m and an Fw 190 on 21 January 1943, a damaged Fw 190 on 29 January 29, two Bf 109s on 20 March, an MC 200 on 13 May and another Bf 109 on eight days later. The two question marks at the right of his scoreboard refer to a pair of Me 210s that collided and crashed when the German formation of five Messerschmitt 'twins' was attacked by Zubarik on 6 May 1943. The pilot was actually heading back to base alone with a malfunctioning engine when he came across the enemy formation, and because there were no other witnesses to the crash, Zubarik was never officially given credit for them.

8

P-38G (serial unknown) *TOMMIE'S/"LUCKY PENNY"* of Lt Sidney W Weatherford, 48th FS/14th FG, North Africa, August 1943

This P-38G was named after Weatherford's wife as a promise to her that he would turn up again after his tour. His aerial victories were all scored over a three-month period from 28 May to 26 August 1943, and included a Bf 109 on 28 May 28, an MC 202 on 12 July, two Ju 52/3ms on 18 July and another Bf 109 on 26 August. Weatherford was one of the first pilots to 'make ace' with the newly-committed 48th FS following the 14th FG's return to the fray in early May 1943 after a fourth-month period of rest and rebuilding.

9

P-38F-15 43-2112/ *"SAD SACK"* of Capt Ernest K Osher, CO of the 95th FS/82nd FG, Berteaux, Algeria, May 1943

Pilots of the 82nd FG claim that this P-38 was made 'absolutely right' by Lockheed, duly giving them something of an edge in combat. As many as 16 confirmed victories, plus several probable and damaged claims, were attributed to *"SAD SACK"* during its long career in the frontline. Although 'Dixie' Sloan scored his first aerial victory in the aircraft on 7 January 1943 (a Bf 109), it was then adopted by Maj Robert Kirtley, and later Maj Ernest Osher, both of whom commanded of the 95th FS for a time during their respective combat tours of North Africa. Kirtley got a Ju 88 and an Ar 196 floatplane in *"SAD SACK"* on 21 February 1943, whilst Lt John Cappo used the fighter to good effect during the rout of Axis transport aircraft on 11 April 1943, claiming two Ju 52/3ms – he also 'bagged' a Bf 109 with the Lightning 18 days later. Five-kill ace Ernest Osher is recorded as having downed his third and fourth victories with *"SAD SACK"* on 5 May 1943, the aircraft subsequently enjoying its final success in the air as late as 13 April 1944 with Flt Off Roland Leeman at the controls – *"SAD SACK"* was damaged by flak and taken out of service soon afterwards.

10

P-38G-15 (serial unknown) *"EARTHQUAKE McGOON"* of Lt Richard A Campbell, 37th FS/14th FG, North Africa, August 1943

Flying with the 37th FS, Campbell was also amongst the elite band of 14th FG pilots to achieve 'acedom' early on in the group's second tour of duty. He scored his first two Bf 109s destroyed (and a third damaged) on 18 May 1943, followed by another Bf 109 as a probable ten days later – the latter score was achieved flying *"EARTHQUAKE McGOON"*. Campbell's third confirmed kill took the form of a MC 202 on 15 June, followed by yet another Bf 109 destroyed on 9 July. He made sure of his ace status with a double Bf 109 score (plus a third fighter damaged) on 28 August 1943. Richard Campbell later completed a second tour in the China-Burma-India (CBI) theatre in 1945, but he failed to add to his tally.

11

P-38G-5 42-12830/ *Snooks IV1/2* of Lt William J 'Dixie' Sloan, 96th FS/82nd FG, Souk-el-Arba, Algeria, July 1943

Sloan became the leading ace of not only the 96th FS/82nd FG, but also the entire Twelfth Air Force, when on 22 July 1943 when he downed a Bf 109 for his 12th victory. This tally would secure him top spot amongst USAAF fighter pilots in the Mediterranean for the next nine months until Mustang pilot Maj Herschel 'Herky' Green claimed his 13th victory for the 325th FG on 7 April 1944 (see *Aircraft of the Aces 7 - Mustang Aces of the Ninth & Fifteenth Air Forces and the RAF* for further details). The nickname *Snooks IV1/2* refers to the fact that so much of this P-38 was made up of spare parts from cannibalised Lightnings that only about half of the aircraft was original! It would seem likely that Sloan used this fighter when he gained his victories during the Sicily invasion period – namely a Bf 109 and a Re 2001 on 5 July and an MC 200 on 10 July 1943.

12

P-38H-5 42-67027 of Lt Gerald A Brown, 38th FS/55th FG, Nuthampstead, November 1943

On 13 November 1943 Jerry Brown (flying this aircraft) and Capt Joe Myers comprised one of the elements put up by the 55th FG to escort bombers on a particularly rough mission to Bremen. The former pilot had already succeeded in damaging an attacking Bf 109 short of the bomber stream when another fighter latched onto his tail and pumped cannon and machine-gun fire into the hapless P-38. Seeing Brown's predicament, Myers managed to shoot the determined German off his colleague's tail, allowing Brown to somehow coax his gravely damaged P-38 home. Once back at Nuthampstead, the bullet-riddled Lightning was the source of much amazement for Lockheed and USAAF technical experts alike, who counted in excess of 100 bullet and cannon hits on the aircraft's fuselage. Flying J-10 model P-38s, Jerry Brown went on to destroy a Bf 109 at high altitude on 31 January 1944, an Fw 190 on 18 March, another Bf 109 on 8 April and a He 111 and a second Fw 190 exactly a week later.

13
P-38H-5 42-67064/*Texas Ranger* of Col Jack Jenkins, Deputy CO 55th FG, Nuthampstead, November 1943

The first victories to fall to the P-38 in north-west Europe were scored by the 55th FG on 3 November 1943, future group commander Jack Jenkins claiming a Bf 109 shot down and an Fw 190 probably destroyed. It would seem from a postwar examination of JG 1's records that Jenkins could actually have claimed both fighters destroyed, as the *Jagdgeschwader* admitted the loss of two fighters in action with P-38s on this day. The colonel tasted success in *Texas Ranger* just once more, using the Lightning to destroy an Fw 190 22 days after his 'double' haul. Jenkins led the first American fighters over Berlin on 3 March 1944 when the 55th FG ranged over the German capitol – his P-38 on this occasion was *Texas Ranger IV*.

14
P-38H (serial unknown) *Stingeree* of Maj William L Leverette, CO 37th FS/14th FG, Gambut-2, Libya, October 1943

Named after a southern American variation of the stingray, this P-38H was used by William Leverette (a native of Florida, hence the 'fishy' nickname) to claim most, if not all, of his 11 aerial victories. The seven Ju 87s that he claimed on 9 October 1943 constituted a record for American pilots in Europe. This astounding tally has often been questioned by ex-pilots and historians alike, but Leverette recently assured the author that one of the P-38 pilots in his formation descended to low altitude over the becalmed sea in order to confirm numerous splashes in the water made by the crashing Stukas. Once the latter individual had returned to base, the number of splashes he reported was consistent with the tally of kills claimed by the successful P-38 pilots. Leverette later destroyed a Bf 109 on 14 December 1943, a Bf 110 on 24 February 1944, another Bf 109 on 18 March and a final Bf 110 on 12 April.

15
P-38G-15 43-2527/*PAT II* of Col Oliver B Taylor, CO of the 14th FG, Triolo, Italy, January 1944

Taylor scored one confirmed kill, one probable and one damaged in this Lightning on 20 December 1943, all three of his foes being Bf 109s encountered during a sweep over Eleusis airfield, in Greece. He gave up *PAT II* towards the end of the following month, receiving a later specification Lightning in its place. The supply problem was always critical in the MTO due to the theatre's distance from the main air depots in Britain. Squadrons were therefore forced use early-build P-38Fs, Gs and Hs for far longer periods than other Lightning outfits in the ETO and Pacific/CBI. After scoring his first successes in December, Col Taylor added a second Bf 109 destroyed to his tally on 10 January and

another Messerschmitt fighter damaged 17 days later. It seems likely that the five scores represented by the victory marks on the side of the fighter's gondola reflect his haul from December and January, for Taylor did not finally achieve 'ace status' until 27 May 1944 whilst flying a P-38J.

16
P-38G-10 42-13480/*Billie-Jo*/NASA *SERBSKA SLO-BODA!*/*Bar Fly* of Lt Donald D Kienholz, 94th FS/1st FG, Italy, January 1944

By the end of January 1944 Kienholz had achieved six confirmed kills and one damaged claim, and like a number of his contemporaries, he used his early-model P-38G for a relatively long time. His first victory was a Bf 109 scored on 13 August 1943 and his last score was also a Messerschmitt fighter, downed on 30 January 1944. Most of his victories were scored during the initial stages of the invasion of Italy, although his last kill in 1943 was an Fw 190 shot down on the same Eleusis airfield sweep on 20 December that Col Oliver Taylor had enjoyed his first combat success. During one strafing mission he had the unnerving experience of being turned upside-down with one flak burst and righted again with the next!

17
P-38J (serial unknown) *Janet* of Capt Thomas A White, 338th FS/55th FG, Wormingford, Spring 1944

White placed the six swastikas on the nose of this 338th FS P-38J even though he had scored all six of his victories with the 97th FS/82nd FG in North Africa between January and March 1943. The aircraft was named after the daughter of the squadron's Intelligence Officer, Wally Ryerson, with whom White maintained a correspondence. Sometime after the captain had left the 338th, the nose of the fighter was painted red (in the same shade as the spinners) through the first two letters of the name. No photos have been found of the P-38 wearing invasion stripes, so it seems likely that the aircraft had been taken out of service before 6 June 1944.

18
P-38J-10 42-67926/*Susie* of Capt Lindol F Graham, 79th FS/20th FG, Kingscliffe, March 1944

The 79th FS was blessed with a number of skilled Lightning pilots, but Capt 'Lindy' Graham was considered to be the 'pick of the bunch'. Rookie pilots looked up to him as the example to follow, for he had been with the unit since its arrival in the frontline, and had scored 5.5 victories in under three months. Thus, when Graham was killed in *Susie* on 18 March 1944, the unit felt it as a body blow. Graham's 'big day' in combat was 29 January, when he downed three Fw 190s in two separate engagements on the same bomber escort mission whilst flying J-10 42-67497. He went on to 'make ace' in the fighter depicted in this profile during a confused aerial clash involving several P-38s and a formation of Bf 110s on 20 February south-west of Brunswick – he claimed two Messerschmitt 'twins' destroyed. The red star painted beneath the fighter's nickname (and the attendant white scroll to its immediate right) was worn in honour of a former Lockheed employee killed in action during World War 2 – these markings were to be found on a number of P-38s, having been carefully applied at the factory immediately prior to the aircraft being delivered to the USAAF. The white Eighth Air Force group recognition symbol on the tail was not added to the P-38 until early March 1944.

19

P-38J-10 42-67717/*My Dad* of Capt James M Morris, 77th FS/20th FG, Kingscliffe, February 1944

Although P-38J-10 42-67717 was the aircraft adorned with 'Slick' Morris's impressive tally, he only claimed one of his 7.333 victories with it – an Me 110 downed over Schweinfurt on 24 February 1944. Morris was the Eighth Air Force's first P-38 ace, and he scored 5.333 of his kills in J-10 42-67871. Four of these came in a single sortie on 8 February 1944, the two Fw 190s and two Bf 109Gs he downed on this mission setting a scoring record at the time for the P-38 in the ETO. Morris got his final kill (an Me 410) in P-38J-15 43-28397 on 7 July 1944, but was in turn so badly shot up by the stricken fighter's remote-controlled waist guns that he too was forced to bale out – he spent the rest of the war as a PoW.

20

P-38J-15 43-104308/*'Gentle Annie'* of Col Harold J Rau, CO of the 20th FG, Kingscliffe, April 1944

Although this machine wears Col Rau's full kill tally, it was not the P-38 he used on 8 April 1944 to lead a last-minute fighter sweep over Germany during which he scored all his victories – and his group won a Distinguished Unit Citation. He managed to down one Bf 109, as well as confirm four unidentified twin-engined aircraft destroyed on the ground during the course of the legendary mission. 20th FG aces Morris and Fiebelkorn also claimed ground victories on this mission. 43-104308 was lost during a strafing mission when hit by flak at Le Treport on 16 June 1944, its pilot, Lt Earl O Smith, managing to evade capture.

21

P-38J-10 42-69166/*Gentle Annie* of Col Harold J Rau, CO of the 20th FG, Kingscliffe, August 1944

Following the loss of the original *Annie*, Rau made use of this P-38J-10 for a brief period, despite the fact the fighter was an older J-10 variant. The aircraft shows signs of having been relieved of its original olive drab (OD) paint scheme – note the OD panel surrounding the gun troughs. It was a highly unusual move for a group commander to choose anything but the latest specification machine operated by the trio of squadrons under his charge for his personal mount, and Rau's decision to fly this veteran J-10 was probably influenced by the fact he was due to become tour-expired in August. In any event, the second *Gentle*

Annie was in service for less than a month before the 20th FG converted to the P-51D Mustang.

22

P-38J-15 42-104107/*JEWBOY* of Lt Philip M Goldstein (now Graham), 49th FS/14th FG, Triolo, Italy, May 1944

Two Jewish pilots within the 49th FS displayed the admirable impudence in decorating their P-38s in defiance of Nazi-oriented Luftwaffe pilots. Lt Robert Seidman placed a large Star of David on the side of his P-38, and duly shot down five German fighters with it before he succumbed to flak during a strafing raid on the airfield at Udine on 14 May 1944. Squadronmate Goldstein (Graham) painted the name *JEWBOY* on the left engine cowling and repeated the taunt in German on the right. He scored his first victory over a Bf 109 on 2 April 1944, and subsequently claimed a Fiat G 50 on 9 May and a Fw 190 16 days later. He also damaged two Bf 109s and destroyed four more aircraft on the ground.

23

P-38J-15 43-28252 of Lt Franklin C Lathrope, 94th FS/1st FG, Italy, May 1944

There was very little in the way of personal identification markings applied to the P-38s of the 1st FG in 1944, five-kill ace Franklin Lathrope's J-15 being typical of the Lightnings flown by the trio of squadrons within the group. Like other aces of the 1st, Lathrope simply accepted any fighter assigned to him for the day, and got on with flying the mission. Number 89 was the aircraft assigned to him on 10 May 1944 when he scored his fourth and fifth victories – two Bf 109s – south of Weiner Neustadt. In point of fact all his victories were Bf 109s, the first being claimed on 11 March 1944, followed by a damaged claim 18 days later, his second confirmed destroyed on 23 April and his fourth on the 29th of the same month.

24

P-38J-15 43-28431/*HAPPY JACK'S GO BUGGY* of Capt Jack M Ilfrey, 79th FS/20th FG, Kingscliffe, May 1944

Although a brilliant pilot, Jack Ilfrey also had a reputation for recklessness both on the ground and in the air. Despite a spell in America after the completion of his first tour in May 1943, his 'history' followed him from the MTO to the ETO when he started his second tour in England with the 79th FS/20th FG in April 1944. Ilfrey tried to live up to his colourful reputation as often as possible, finding his various escapades (and the subsequent punishments) the best release for the tension of daily air combat. His two aerial victories with the 79th FS came whilst flying this J-15 on 24 May 1944 during a bomber escort to Berlin. Ilfrey climbed into the Bf 109 top cover and shot one down at 30,000 ft before inadvertently ramming a second, losing about four feet of wing and sending the German fighter down in flames. Although he survived this mission, Ilfrey went down in this same fighter on 13 June 1944 when it was hit by fire during an a strafing mission on the airfield at Angers, in France. He managed to evade capture and returned to Kingscliffe, where he served firstly as Operations Officer and then CO of the 79th FS from 27 September to 9 December 1944.

25
P-38J-15 4?-??328/Mon Amy of Lt Herbert B Hatch, 71st FS/1st FG, Italy, June 1944

Despite having accrued little combat experience during the first two months of his tour with the 1st FG, Lt 'Stub' Hatch showed just how effective the stateside training for fighter pilots was when he downed five Romanian I.A.R.80s (misidentified as Fw 190s at the time) during the ill-fated Ploesti mission of 10 June 1944. His only previous taste of aerial combat had come on 6 May when he shared in the probable destruction of a Bf 109 with another 71st FS pilot. Hatch's official tally for the 10 June mission was five aircraft downed, one probably destroyed and another damaged. His first three victories were captured by his gun camera before the film broke, whilst the others were confirmed by downed 71st FS pilots (Hatch was the only pilot to make it back to base with his P-38) who later turned up.

26
P-38J-10 42-68024/SNOOKIE II of Lt Jack Lenox, 49th FS/14th FG, Triolo, Italy, June 1944

Lenox was a firebrand who confirmed five enemy aircraft destroyed and a probable, plus three additional damaged claims, within a six-month span. His first confirmed victory was a Bf 109 scored on 23 May 1944, which was followed up less than 24 hours later by a Me 210, and then a damaged Bf 109 on the 25th. Lenox 'made ace' during a big battle involving the 14th FG over Petfurdo, in Hungary, on 14 June 1944, the P-38 pilot claiming three Bf 109s shot down.

27
P-38J-15 43-28650/SWEET SUE/NELLIE ANN of Lt Phillip E Tovrea, 27th FS/1st FG, Italy, June 1944

Tovrea was the scion of a wealthy family who decided to do his bit for his country by becoming an ace with the 27th FS in 1944! He used 43-28650 very rarely, scoring kills in at least four other P-38Js, although he managed to claim two Bf 109s in this fighter on 16 June 1944. Tovrea's most productive day came on 18 July 1944 when he downed two Fw 190s and a Bf 109, and damaged a further two Focke-Wulfs, while flying P-38J-15 43-28734. His final score was eight confirmed, one probable and three damaged.

28
P-38J-15 42-104096 of Capt Thomas E Maloney, 27th FS/1st FG, Italy, May 1944

Being squadronmates, Maloney and Tovrea often flew on the same missions, and apparently enjoyed a mutual respect for one another. Much like Tovrea, Tom Maloney flew whatever fighter was available on the day, but remembers J-15 43-28746 #23 as his usual

mount. He used the P-38 featured here in profile on 28 May 1944 to down a Do 217 over Buxim, in Yugoslavia, and a Bf 109 over Ploesti three days later. Maloney's final tally of eight kills was comprised of four Bf 109s, two Bf 110s, an Fw 190 and a Do 217.

29
P-38J-15 43-28796/Judy Ann of Lt Charles E Adams, 95th FS/82nd FG, Vincenzo, Italy, June 1944

Although Adams used this P-38 as his own mount, all bar one of his six victories were scored in other aircraft. Judy Ann's sole success took the form of a Bf 110 downed east of Vienna on 26 June 1944, the pilot's remaining scores being achieved in P-38G-10 42-13199 (Me 210) on 13 April, P-38J-15 43-28654 (Fw 190) on 16 June and P-38J-15 44-23188 (three Me 410s) on 8 July – the 95th FS claimed six Messerschmitt 'twins', plus five other types, on this mission over Vienna. So one-sided was the action that the squadron debriefing officers had to stop the pilots' claims when more they exceeded the entire total of the enemy formation! Judy Ann was the name Adams's daughter.

30
P-38J-15 43-28746 of Capt Thomas E Maloney, 27th FS/1st FG, Italy, August 1944

Maloney scored his final two kills (both Bf 109s) in this P-38 on 15 August 1944. Having met Tom Maloney on several occasions, the author finds it hard to imagine this exceptionally agreeable person finding enough aggression within him to destroy or damage a dozen enemy in aerial combat. The truth of the matter is that he was tough enough to tangle with Luftwaffe veterans on a more than equal footing, plus make a full recovery from horrendous injuries suffered when he trod on a land mine on the coast of southern France after being shot down on 19 August 1944. Despite his wounds, Maloney managed to evade the enemy for a number of days before finally being rescued.

31
P-38J-10 42-68008/Touché of Lt Col James Herren, CO of the 434th FS/479th FG, Wattisham, June 1944

A popular commander, Herren led the 434th FS during its first months with the Eighth Air Force from May through to September 1944. This unit provided three of the 479th FG's four aces, all of whom had been led with deftness and determination by Herren during their first crucial combat sorties. He scored all his P-38 aerial victories on 26 September 1944 when the 479th garnered 29 confirmed claims for just a single loss. Herren also claimed a Ju 52/3m on the ground and shared a stationary He 111 with another pilot when the group destroyed a number of aircraft during a series of strafing runs on 18 August 1944. He was finally killed in action in a P-51D during yet another ground attack mission in October 1944. P-38J-10 Touché was unusual in sporting a black ID disc on its twin tails, for the 434th FS had previously used a white triangle on its OD

Lightnings and the 435th the circle marking – perhaps this aircraft had been 'acquired' from the latter unit at some point. The squadron painter hated the tedium of accurately masking off the tail symbols, and he was quite pleased when the 434th adopted to the simple all-red rudder marking in August 1944.

32
P-38J-25 44-23677/ "LITTLE BUCKAROO" of Maj Robert C 'Buck' Rogers, CO of the 392nd FS/367th FG, Peray, France, August 1944

As mentioned in chapter six, the J-25 model of the P-38, with its hydraulically-boosted ailerons and under-wing divebrakes, arrived in the ETO too late to see service with the Eighth 8th Air Force, but *was* extensively employed by the three P-38 groups of the Ninth Air Force towards the end of 1944. The J-25 was not only the fastest version of the P-38, but also the most manoeuvrable. Maj 'Buck' Rogers was another popular commander, who led the 392nd FS with fairness and competence according to those who served with him. All his victories were scored on the ground during a single mission on 25 August 1944, Rogers being credited with five Ju 52/3ms destroyed on an airfield near Dijon, in France. As previously mentioned, the Ninth Air Force did not grant individual credits for aircraft destroyed on the ground, thus Rogers is an unofficial ace.

33
P-38J-15 43-28341/ SCAT II of Capt Robin Olds, 434th FS/479th FG, Wattisham, August 1944

This P-38 was one of the few in the 434th FS that retained an olive drab camouflage scheme right up until the type was replaced by the P-51D in late September 1944. Fred Hayner began the squadron practice of painting the rudder red in place of the geometric symbol on the tail, and aside from this marking, and the aircraft's nickname, there is no photographic evidence of any other personal or official embellishments to Olds's P-38 except in the memory of the former individual. Olds himself remembers nothing of his Lightning, other than the general squadron codes ('L2-W') and the name SCAT on the nose. Hayner fortunately used standard markings throughout the squadron, 'his' aircraft being the most distinctively marked of all 479th FG P-38s.

34
P-38J-25 44-23590/ SCRAPIRON IV of Capt Lawrence E Blumer, CO of the 393rd FS/367th FG, Juvincourt, France, November 1944

Blumer was one of the more 'enthusiastic' fighter pilots within the 394th FS/367th FG, his aircraft being given the nickname SCRAPIRON in view of the condition that he often brought them back to base in. He managed to claim five Fw 190 fighters shot down on 25 August 1944 while coming to the rescue of his comrades during a strafing mission (it is uncertain whether he was flying this aircraft at the time). The Fw 190 unit involved in the action was the relatively new JG 6,

which admitted the loss of 16 fighters in its daily records, while the P-38 group claimed 20 victories. Blumer scored one more Fw 190 kill in November, but marked his final P-38 with a row of seven swastikas, possibly indicating a sixth aged Fw 190 that he damaged during the course of his record haul on 25 August. He finished his tour as CO of the 393rd FS, having led the unit from November 1944 to January 1945.

35
P-38J-15 42-104425/ BOOMERANG of Capt Arthur F Jeffrey, 343rd FS/479th FG, Wattisham, August 1944

Another 434th FS ace who started his scoring in the P-38 and finished it with the P-51D/K, Jeffrey claimed his first four kills between 5 July (a rare Fw 200 Condor, downed over Cognac/Chateaubernard airfield) and 28 August 1944 (a Ju 52/3m, claimed over Sedan/Douzy airfield). The reason for the fifth cross, applied slightly to the left of the remaining four victory symbols, remains unexplained, unless Jeffrey anticipated confirmation of a victory which subsequently did not become recorded in any way (confirmed, probable or damaged). The second of Jeffrey's confirmed Lightning haul took the form of an Me 163 rocket interceptor, engaged over Wilhelmshaven on 29 July 1944 in this very P-38. It is interesting to speculate just how the combat would have gone if he had been using a J-25 model, for although Jeffrey was given a destroyed credit, it is now believed that his foe managed to land with substantial battle damage. Having risen to command the 434th FS by the end of his tour, Jeffrey scored a further ten kills in the Mustang to make him the group's leading wartime ace.

36
P-38J-25 (serial unknown) of Lt Lawrence P Liebers, 429th FS/474th FG, Langensalza, June 1945

Liebers was assigned to the 474th FG soon after VE-Day and received this 'clean' P-38. With hostilities over, he thus ended the war with seven confirmations gained with the 96th FS/82nd FG in North Africa in 1943 – five of these were Italian aircraft, this tally being the highest scored by a USAAF pilot. No markings other than unit or national were apparent on photos of this aircraft, suggesting that the fighter was extremely clean at least when Liebers began using it in the late spring of 1945. With no more action to be seen, Liebers, and many other P-38 pilots for the group, transferred out in July an ended up flying C-47s instead. Having survived so much action in World War 2, Larry Liebers was killed in an AT-7C Navigator accident in California on 21 August 1946.

37
P-38J-15 43-28474/ GIVE 'M HELL - FOR H L of Capt Claire A P Duffie, 434th FS/479th FG, Wattisham, September 1944

Another 'combined' ace from the 434th FS, Duffie

claimed three Bf 109s in the air and two other ground victories mostly in this P-38. The reason for the distinctive inscription on the nose is known only to Duffie. This P-38 was finally retired from service, still with the remnants of its D-Day stripes intact, around 28 September 1944 when the 479th FG completed its transition to the P-51D.

38
P-38J-25 44-23624/*LES VIN, LES FEMMES, LES CHANSONS* of Capt Paul J Sabo, 485th FS/370th FG, Lonray, October 1944

The French phrase that comprises the name of this P-38 indicates the mentality of most young American pilots – 'wine, women and song'. Paul Sabo accounted for 1/3 of a Fw 200 with the 77th FS/20th FG on 5 February 1944 and an Fw 190 with the 485th FS/370th FG on 20 October 1944. The tally on the nose of the P-38 indicates that Sabo was sure of more than his official victories, being credited with four other aircraft destroyed or damaged.

39
P-38J-15 43-28258/*Pat III* of Col Oliver B Taylor, CO of the 14th FG, Triolo, Italy, July 1944

Col Taylor kept his P-38J-15 with the 49th FS during his time as CO of the 14th FG. There is no record that he scored any victories in this particular fighter, although Wilson H Oldhouse claimed an Fw 190 while flying it on 11 June 1944. Taylor was struck down with polio at about this time and eventually transferred out of the group on 17 July, command having since transferred to Col Daniel Campbell.

40
P-38J-25 42-??663/*SWAT* of Lt Robert C Milliken, 429th FS/474th FG, Florennes, Belgium, October 1944

Milliken became one of the last P-38 aces in the ETO when he claimed a Bf 109 on 18 December 1944 near Köln. His first victories in this P-38J-25 were probably the two Fw 190s that he claimed on 12 September 1944 near Aachen – a further three remained unconfirmed damaged. All the P-38J-25s illustrated in invasion markings must have been early examples that operated from airfields just inland from the Normandy beaches, since there was little chance that the sub-type could have reached any operational areas by 6 June 1944. *SWAT* was Milliken nickname.

—— FIGURE PLATES ——

1
Col Oliver Taylor, CO of the 14th FG at Triolo, in Italy, in the spring of 1944, is seen wearing lightweight khaki 'pinks' (uniform khaki trousers) with an open-necked matching shirt, over which he has donned a well-worn A-2 jacket, minus rank tabs. His life preserver is a small and snug B-3, whilst his helmet is an RAF-issue Type D – the British helmet was renowned for not only giving better ear protection than its American equivalent, but also improved radio clarity due both to its deeper ear cups and better sealing around the ears themselves. The mask attached to the highly-prized helmet is a USAAF standard issue A-10, as are the B-7 goggles. Finally, Taylor has A-6A single-strap boots on his feet.

2
Lt Richard A Campbell flew with the 37th FS/14th FG in North Africa in 1943, and he is seen wearing typically improvised flying gear synonymous with the theatre. His trousers are khaki paratrooper issue (note combat webbing), whilst his shirt is standard USAAF rig, with sleeves permanently rolled up – these cotton shirts were comfortable to wear, although they stayed permanently creased once worn due to the combination of sweat and heat. His life preserver is again a B-3, to which he has attached a map board, which is also tied around his right thigh. Campbell's helmet is a Type D, with the headset itself exposed – the goggles are B-7s. He is holding a full B-8 parachute pack.

3
Lt William 'Dixie' Sloan of the 96th FS/82nd FG, as he appeared at Grombalia, Tunisia, in September 1943. He is attired in standard-issue khaki shirt and trousers, with a heavily-stained B-3 life preserver worn over his chest. Sloan carries a Colt .45 in a shoulder holster, with an associated magazine pouch clipped to his waist belt – note too the sunglasses case just above it.

4
Lt Claude Kinsey of the 96th FS/82nd FG in North Africa in March 1943. Again he is wearing 'pinks', although these are tucked into RAF 1940 Pattern flying boots. Kinsey's sheepskin-lined jacket is a heavy B-3, pirated from a bomber crewman, whilst his cap has felt the effect of the much-prized '50 mission crush'.

5
Capt 'Lindy' Graham of the 79th FS/20th FG at Kingscliffe in September 1943. The future ace is wearing woollen OD trousers (turned up rather than tucked into his Russet GI issue boots) and a B-10 jacket, minus its fur collars. Beneath his khaki jacket, Graham has on an officers' issue khaki shirt and matching tie, the former complete with rank tabs. His helmet is again ex-RAF, although this time it's an earlier Type C – the attached goggles are USAAF B-7s, as are the pilot's B-2 gloves. Finally, his parachute pack is a B-8.

6
Lt James Morris of the 77th FS/20th FG at Kingscliffe in February 1944. He is wearing a US Army tank crewman's winter jacket and bib overalls, over which a ubiquitous B-3 life preserver has been donned. His gloves are fur-lined gauntlet style A-9s, his helmet/goggles combination identical to Lindol Graham's and his mask an A-10. Finally, his uniform is completed by a pair of heavy A-2A single-strap flying boots – and a white neck scarf!